Confessions of a

Feel Good Addict

How to escape the pitfalls of the comfort zone

and live a life on purpose

By

Michele A. Lewis

"This is a thought-provoking book that challenges the reader to really look deep into themselves and examine areas that may be preventing them from being or doing what they are meant to be or do. It 'speaks' to the mentally inquisitive mind as well as the emotional mind. It provides a great balance in explaining interesting scientific studies in understandable terms with sharing transparent stories/examples from her own life experiences. It's like scientific journal meets novelist." – Murphy Boughner, Former High School Drug and Alcohol Counselor

"Engaging, challenging, funny and relevant. Michele opens her heart and soul in a non-judgmental, vulnerable and witty way… The book has an easy flow, is insightful and full of life nuggets and great questions. If you are stuck in a rut and need a nudge to get you moving in the right direction, this book is for you. Excellent read!" – Angela. Shilley, Accounting Professional - Richmark Inc.

"Our wheel of life is made up of our work, relationships, health, finances, environment and spiritual sections. Michele has touched on each of these areas of our life to shine a light on where we may have become complacent as a "feel good addict". What I love about this book is Michele's own confessions; she is a work in progress! Like all of us! Her research and facts support her findings and most importantly I found her suggestions genuine either to implement or questions to reflect on." – Barb Avery, Trainer & Coach -In Full Bloom Leadership

"Thought provoking and behavior changing! I've never thought about putting meaning into things and doing it subconsciously and how it can affect what we do. Michele has done her research and written a well-rounded book! I couldn't put it down. I hope she writes many more books as I will be one of the first in line to read them!" – Laurie Brown, Benefits Analyst - Rael & Letson

ISBN-13: 978-1545531631
ISBN-10: 1545531633

Dedication

This book is for all who have like me, struggled with being stuck in the comfort zone, the cyclic nightmare of status quo or have given up or given in to a life that is only 'good enough'. It is my hope that this book becomes a lifeline to lift you out and set you free.

I also dedicate this book to those who haven't yet discovered they are stuck. May they experience illuminating freedom!

Pam

Blessings!

Philippians 4:13

Acknowledgements

I thank my dear friend Mila Reid for rattling my cage one painfully honest day, shaking me loose from my self-imposed dismal forebodings that laid the foundation for this book. To Patricia "Murphy" Boughner for her consistent encouragement over the many long, tedious years that were full of kind-hearted and sometimes prodding conversations – it made the journey full and blessed. A special thanks to two Angela's in my life. Angela Shilley, for the many interesting conversations, stories and adventures over the years that still make me laugh and contributed to bringing context to some of the stories in this book. To Angela Craig, a new and timely friend whose leadership and grace filled life has been an inspiration and guide to help me find balance.

Most of all, I thank my God and Savior, Jesus Christ. Without Him, this book and my life, would not be in existence.

Table of Contents

Introduction 1

Origins of the Feel Good Addict 4

Why We Do What We Do 21

Our Health 32

Our Finances 47

Career and Purpose 55

Relationships 66

Home and Pets 76

Relationship with God 85

Conclusion 101

How I Did It 104

Bible Reading Plan 106

Introduction

The concept for this book emerged after listening to a friend ramble on daily about how she hated her job, yet didn't seem interested in exploring any solutions.

After hearing her share about her employment misery, I reflected on a time in my own life where I was that very same person. I felt trapped in an oppressive job. I was complaining every day, and for some reason I couldn't see a way out. It was as if I was blinded and imprisoned, unable to free myself. My eyes weren't opened until a good friend, sick of hearing my incessant whining, literally verbally slapped me upside the head. This person simply said: "If you don't like it, leave. Otherwise, shut up." Those may sound like harsh words, but it was the best advice I ever got. It freed me from the trappings of self-victimization.

Eventually my other friend had her eyes opened as well. Reflections on these situations sparked what felt like divine inspiration. It led me to unpack what seemed to be a phenomenon, not just in my generation, but actually throughout history. A phenomenon of people being sucked into the status quo and the dull rhythms of life. People settling for good enough. Being okay to drift into the trappings of the comfort zone, and oddly satisfied to stay there. I have named this pandemic affecting us all: *the feel good addiction.*

This addiction is about avoiding discomfort. It's about being drawn into the trap of pleasure-seeking with an unquenchable thirst. It's about never being satisfied.

It doesn't appear the same for everyone. For some people it is quite obvious, for others it is covert. It could be an employee more comfortable in the discomfort of a miserable job. Or a person who really wants to lose weight, but can't seem to stay away from the treats. It's a woman settling for an abusive relationship, believing it is better than no relationship. A man paralyzed in a purposeless life, because pursuing his dream feels too far out of reach. It's the family that never has enough money to pay the bills, but can't stop buying things. The husband and wife whose relationship has gone cold, but are too tired to light the flame. It's the pet that sits outside alone, crying, because its owner is too busy with their own life to notice. It's you, and it's me.

Lured by the deception of self-satisfaction and instant gratification, our lives slowly erode as the feel good addiction within seduces us for more pleasure and greater avoidance of discomfort. When we collectively are trapped in this addiction, it has power to impact our communities and our world in profound ways.

This pleasure-seeking drive can paralyze (or cost) a life and destroy relationships, careers and homes. Many are not even aware they have this addiction because it is a learned way of living. With roots dating back to the dawn of time, this addiction has become part of our internal wiring and is a trap that slowly tears us down until there doesn't seem to be a way out.

This book is about turning on the light to expose the deceptive force of this addiction in all of us, and illuminating the way to escape it and stay free. The bulk of the book will include sections of how this addiction affects our health, wealth and sense of purpose. It will examine how it affects our careers, our relationships, our home (including our pets), and our relationship with God. It will explore where the feel good addiction got its start, how it has evolved, and why it has been so hard to break its hold.

As you read, you will undoubtedly start to recognize patterns of your own feel good addiction from the 'confessions' and stories woven throughout the pages. For this, I have included short tailored questions in each chapter to help you make shifts in your thinking and practical easy-to-apply tools that will result in positive changes in your actions. Awareness is what brings about change. As we become aware we gain strength, courage and wisdom to overcome and be freed from the comfort zone and the feel good addiction.

This book is for everyone.

If you are ready to get real, get honest, have a bit of fun and experience transformation, turn the page and let's get started. This book will be your biggest cheerleader, and your most honest best friend.

Origins of the Feel Good Addict

Have you ever wondered where the phrase, "If it feels good do it" came from? I always thought it was from the sixties, but it actually dates back further in some form or another. Before we dive into why we become feel good addicts, it is important to understand the origins of this phenomenon and see how it has evolved into where we are today. History has a way of helping us understand the 'how,' as in how we got where we are.

This chapter will give you an overview of where this phenomenon started and how it evolved over the centuries, concluding with a cultural snapshot of where we are today. The very last part of this chapter will give you an opportunity to take your own mini personal snapshot of where you are at, so that when you finish this book you will be able to see how your awareness has increased and the areas where you have changed. The next chapter will dive into why we do what we do and how we are programmed this way.

In the 1960s the phrase, "If it feels good, do it," was chanted by men, women and children. It was an era of free love, free thinking and free doing—no matter who or what was affected by it. As much as the 60s and Woodstock get blamed (or takes credit) for this 'free living' concept, it actually has origins far earlier than that. Clear back to the beginning of time. The first incidence actually occurs in the Bible, in the Garden of Eden. You might know the story. The one where the mother of all humanity pined after the infamous apple? The lovely red, juicy and tasty-looking fruit that she was told not to touch. It was the apple that the crafty serpent deceived her into eating by telling her a lie. God had told Adam and Eve not to eat of that tree or they would die. But the serpent said, surely you won't die—in fact by eating it, they would be like God, knowing all things!

I'm thinking that Eve might have had a moment of saying to the serpent, "Seriously? How cool is that!" What a pretty enticing opportunity! Who wouldn't want to know all things? She saw that it looked good, so she took a bite. Then she called over to her hubby and said "Hey, try this." While they both enjoyed this new taste, suddenly, a newfound knowledge entered their consciousness: "Oh crap, were naked!" Then they hid!

What followed was heartbreaking. God asked them why they were hiding and they replied because they were naked. God asked them, "Who told you that you were naked?" It is the dialog next that we see the first instance of justification by the feel good addict play out. The blame game began with Adam saying the woman YOU (God) gave me, gave it to me to eat. Eve followed with, the serpent YOU (God) put in the garden, told me to eat it.

This is the first historical and biblical account of truth and consequences recorded. Because of the deception, the serpent was cursed to crawl on its belly and eat dust forever. Eve was to experience painful childbearing and Adam would work his fingers to the bone tending the ground. On top of that, everyone was evicted out of the garden paradise.

Before that, they didn't have to work. They didn't have to worry about clothes or food or weather. It was like winning a lifetime lottery. Everything was in beautiful balance and harmonious community with the Creator and His creations. This was the first deception of the feel good addict. Adam and Eve truly did experience death. Their physical death didn't happen when they took the bite as the serpent made them believe. But it did eventually happen. They were created to live forever. The first pleasure deception cost them their life and a comfortable life with the Creator of all things. That was one bad apple.

One bad choice led to a lifetime of living out the consequences and it affected others immediately. God took the life of innocent animals to get skin to clothe them. It was the first sacrifice to cover over man's mess ups. The biggest and most permanent sacrifice was when God sent His son Jesus to die on the cross for all of us, once and for all, clothed and covered.

Now maybe your feel good addict is thinking those consequences over one apple sure seems pretty harsh. Much like my friend who challenged me to leave my job or shut up, sometimes hearing, seeing, and facing the hard truth about ourselves and situations is rather harsh and even painful. But the truth is always meant to protect us, to set us free from the trapping of deception and half-truths. For instance, if you told someone they would burn their fingers if they touched the fire, but they touched it anyway, burning their hands, is the fire being harsh? Was the person who gave the warning being truthful or mean? No matter how much we want to avoid feeling the discomfort and pain of our choices, sometimes there is just no other alternative available.

Let's fast forward a few hundred years to the story of Noah and the massive flood. It's the biblical account of the flood that wiped all things off the face of the earth, (except a few handpicked survivors alongside pairs of the exotic creatures of the world) on a giant boat. The bible describes humanity during the time of Noah as being bent toward doing nothing but evil. Evil is merely the absence of good. If we don't know what good is, then we can't see what evil is. Mankind was increasingly bent toward "doing what was right in their own eyes."[1] Translation? If it feels good, do it—and not necessarily what was good for them or others. Not only were they now aware they were naked and needed to be covered, they were really messing their lives up. Murdering at will, family conflicts, power struggles over riches and kingdoms, competitive self-grandeur and every man and woman pursuing anything and everything that seemed right to them. God got to a point where he had seen enough. He was heartbroken that man just wouldn't listen or learn from their past mistakes. (Remember the apple incident?). No, they just kept insisting on doing their own thing and not only messing up their lives, but impacting the lives of generations to come.

So God gave the world a bath. Whoosh. Gone. A new start. A clean canvas. Except for the handful of vagabond castaways and their pets, everything was gone. Noah and his family were responsible for restarting our population, and as the population grew, old ways from before the flood started to re-emerge. That was to be expected. After all, they were blood relatives from the same family of origin, Adam and Eve. They all spoke the same language and God commanded them to go and populate the earth. Instead however, they decided to stay and be united in one place to secure their own position on

---

[1] The bible, NLT Judges 17:6

earth, self-protecting and staying comfortable. The GO out THERE was big, vast and scary!

In what must have been an epiphany of assumed brilliance, mankind had the brilliant idea to build a tower to reach the heavens. Why not? Sounds reasonable to me. They thought 'now how cool it would be to put their name on it and be infamous, powerful, and invincible'. The lure to do whatever felt good to them in the moment, despite what was ideal, practical or even logical, and continued on with construction. God is so patient with mankind. Instead of another flood, God confused their language so they would finely scatter and populate the earth. They no longer knew how to communicate or relate. They slowly dissipated to where they were really meant to go. In essence they did become famous. God called the tower the 'Tower of Babel'… because He caused mankind to babble their language. The word babel actually means, according to Webster's Dictionary, "a confused noise, typically made by a number of voices". It's ironic how we too can get messed up and confused and staying stuck when we listen to a number of voices all telling us to go, do and be what is not who we are meant to be.

When we stay in a pattern of doing what we want, with and to whomever we want, tossing responsibility, consequences or care for others aside, well, that pretty much messes up the delicate balance of living in community with one another.

It was the same thing but different circumstances from our first story of Adam and Eve. Imagine if Eve hadn't sought to satisfy her craving for the shiny red apple? Or if man had merely spread out like they were told? We'd have no language barriers. No racial conflicts. And quite possibly, everyone getting along. But thinking about consequences wasn't in the forefront, because once the enticement occurred and the mother of all peoples and nations gave into her feel good addict it set the baseline for all that came after her.

Several thousand years later, in the year 1532, François Rabelais' wrote a series of satire novels about two giants named Gargantua and Pantagruel. It is a raucous depiction of fun-loving, free-eating, hard-drinking, let's-stay-merry giants whose mantras were simply "Do as thou wilt."[2] Although comical, it depicted the depravity of the day. This was a time that was emerging out of the middle ages, or more commonly known, the Age of Discovery. This time period included extensive European overseas exploration and the beginning of globalization and colonization, into what we know now as the United States. The world was on a fast pace to expand, control and legalize many of the feel good ways of living. Prostitution, racism, gender demeaning and manipulated and calculated murders were included in the outcome.

In 1904, English occultist Aleister Crowley wrote in his book, "The Book of the Law", (a writing allegedly given to him from a supernatural entity named Aiwass) the words he stated were divinely inspired by this entity - that for man to find their true will in life, they should "do as thou wilt."

German Chancellor Adolf Hitler instigated the mass annihilation of millions of Jews in the 1940s, exercising his definition of doing 'as he wilt.' In 1953, Wiccan Gerald Gardener[3] wrote a journal called the "Gardnerian Book of

---

[2] Rabelais, François. *Gargantua and Pantagruel*. Everyman's Library. ISBN 978-0-679-43137-4

[3] Gerald Brosseau Gardner (1884-1964) has been called the father of

Shadows - The Old Laws-Sacred Texts." In his writing he added a second part to the "do as thou wilt" statement saying "so long as it harms no other". This theme then ushered us into the Sixties, but the latter part of that statement has been more of a politically correct theory than a practice.

In the sixties birth control was created as a means to limit childbirth without limiting the pleasure frequency. In the 70s abortion was legalized for those who weren't so fortunate to prevent a pregnancy with birth control. This also was the decade of coming out of the closet as New York saw the first Gay Pride parade. Do as thou wilt was taking on new and grandeur meaning in the American culture. Fun, free living and merriment, however continued to produce catastrophic consequences.

The 80s wasn't just the big hair era. It announced the first recognized case of AIDS by the Center of Disease Control in the United States. This disease seemed isolated at the time to only male homosexuals. By 1986 however, over 1 million Americans had been infected and in 10 years, that grew to over 5 million. It also affected drug users and the unsuspecting souls receiving transfusions of what they thought was life-giving blood donated by thousands who were unknowingly infected.

In 1960, 292 documented illegal abortions were performed. Throughout the entire decade of the 70's after abortion was legalized, 193,491 were performed. At the end of the 80s a total

---

modern Wicca. His published works are supposedly the teachings of a coven in which he was a member--teachings passed down by word of mouth since early pagan times. Along with his written legacy, he was also the founder of the Museum of Witchcraft.

of 14,182,380 abortions were performed in the United States alone.

Roe v. Wade (US Supreme Court, 410 U.S. 113, (1973)) stimulated research into how to perform legal abortions more safely, protecting the mothers but unfortunately not the contents in their womb. This is not a debate about fetus vs. baby, or women's rights vs. men's rights, rape victims vs. consensual sex. It is merely to stay true to our theme of the impact of our actions affecting others. Something or someone got harmed in this process to satisfy the desires of another. The purpose of abortion was to relieve the burden of the unwanted consequences of an unintended pregnancy or botched birth control practices—whether by choice or fault is not the discussion. It is honestly stating that the engaging in a consensual sexual act without consideration of the repercussions (if it feels good, do it) affects more than the impregnated woman regardless of how it is defined.

In the late 70's, a sudden reversal began to take center stage. The theme became more "If it feels good, DON'T do it." In fact, during Jimmy Carter's term as president the new mantra was "If it feels good, it must be risky and bad, immoral, and dangerous to your health."[4] This new mantra stirred up quite a bit of controversy and rebellion, even though there was a great deal of truth to it.

In the 90s and into the present, the United States has seen a surge in obesity, diabetes and heart disease. Alcoholism began to rise in extreme numbers as did alcohol-related motor vehicle

---

[4] Richard Klien, NY Times,
http://www.nytimes.com/1996/07/28/books/if-it-feels-good-don-t-do-it.html

accidents. A second destructive consequence of the feel good addict began skyrocketing alongside alcoholism – drug-related deaths.

Taking center stage, the once secretive fad of pornography flew out in the open as advocates cited freedom of speech to make it more publicly available. Although abortion began to slightly decline, homosexuality was becoming more public, and not just among men anymore. Bullying, racism and gender inequality were still alive and well, just more covertly masked under politically correct terminology.

Pulitzer Prize-winning writer and critic David Shaw noted in his book The Pleasure Police that "life is a feast, not an endurance test.[5]" He defended the desires of pleasure seekers everywhere to be kept free and to put an end to the extreme left and right zealots from ruining the fun-loving pleasures of everyone else.[5] He also said that "in American culture, all universal sources of pleasure are eventually medicalized, then politicized, and finally policed (if not prohibited). Alcohol, tobacco, cannabis, fat, pornography, masturbation, perfume, all things Shaw calls "policing puritanism.[5]" He cites it to be nothing more than envy "that fuels the puritans to take away the freedoms to indulge to any excess desirable to the individual.[5]" Alas, some honesty from a feel good addict.

At the turn of the century and during the subsequent 10 years, we entered into a whole new era of feel good addicts: terrorists. Doing what was right in their own eyes, and as they

---

[5] The Pleasure Police: How Bluenose Busybodies and Lily-Livered Alarmists Are Taking All the Fun Out of Life. By David Shaw. 1996 307 pp. New York: https://www.amazon.com/Pleasure-Police-David-Shaw/dp/0385475683

willed, Al-Qaeda terrorists killed over 3,000 Americans in one day in 2001. In 2002, Indonesia experienced their worst terrorist attack in their history. Train bombings in Spain and massive suicide bombings in England and Iraq topped the news coverage. What was not-so-top of news that decade was that another tower to reach the heavens was being built. The Burj Khalifa or Burj Dubai is the tallest man made building in the world standing at 2,717 feet. This hotel tower was erected in Dubai in the midst a great deal of controversy. I wonder how tall the tower of Babel was.

Beginning in the next decade, the first of many Occupy Wall Street protesters gathered in downtown New York City and began to protest perceived undue influence of big corporations, greed, and corruption. In their freedom of expression, the freedoms of others were affected during their protests.

In 2014, a new terrorist group called ISIS (a rebranded Al Qaeda) fueled headline news that continues through to the present. A group that takes what they want, when they want, and killing whomever they want - innocent men, women and children - it makes no difference.

In 2015 same sex marriage became legal nationwide. In the name of the freedom to marry, the freedom to disagree was made illegal, taking away, in some cases, the livelihood from those who refused to exercise their freedom of choice to not associate or accommodate. Calling it discrimination while discriminating. Real discrimination is a feel good addict behavior. Doing as we will, regardless of who it affects. Riots, profiling, unprovoked murders and forcing others to accept, participate or celebrate another's idea of freedom are merely masked expressions of the self-serving, self-focused feel good addict. To live in community requires compromise and respect mutually.

It's now 2017. The expressions of the feel good addict are taking on a whole new spin. Laws are being enacted granting freedoms or expression to some, at the expense of silencing others. Shaw's concern about the pleasure police taking away the fun of the indulgent few has taken a 180 degree twist. The very people who seek to maintain that which brings them pleasure do so at an increasing cost to others. Pornography, substance abuse, obesity and out-of-control gambling has increased, destroying families, financial stability and lives. These are nothing but bondage masquerading as freedoms.

Gender confusion has been on the rise as gender fluidity has become the *gender du jour* in our media, schools and governments. The consequences and ramifications affecting children who are not able to form healthy attachments with their parents has contributed to the increased confusion. More and more children are left emotionally and developmentally on their own to sort out who is really safe to bond with, how to successfully navigate their gender development and what are appropriate social and behavioral actions within community. Granted, often this is not unavoidable due to the need for parents to work. It is not the need to work that is being referred to. It's the time outside of work. Parents get tired. It's easier and more convenient to satisfy the parental feel good addict by sitting a child in front of the television, video game or in the care of another than it is to engage in relationship. Parenting is a privilege not an obligation.

In today's climate, mental disorders in children and adults has risen to epidemic proportions. The World Health Organization is trying hard to keep up. The Diagnostic and

Statistical Manual of Mental Disorders (DSM), an official guide responsible for aiding psychiatrists and medical professionals in making clinical diagnoses, added 15 new disorders in its latest release including hoarding, binge eating, internet addiction, and hypersexual disorders. They could easily lump all of them into one category. Feel good addiction.

Children are learning this well from their elder role models. The rise of children emancipating themselves or murdering their parents over things like taking away privileges or for simply telling them no is a great example of do as I do, not as I say.

I once had an employee who had just graduated high school tell me that the word 'no' was negative and shouldn't be spoken. He said his teacher reinforced that in his classroom. He was not being sarcastic but serious and to him, NO felt traumatic. It took discussion and sensitivity to explain to an eighteen year old that no can be just a positive as yes in the right circumstances. I wondered why that discussion wasn't done at his home. Author Henry Cloud of the book *Boundaries* stated that "when parents teach children that setting boundaries or saying no is bad, they are teaching them that others can do with them as they wish, and are sending their children defenseless into a world that contains so much evil". It also teaches them that setting boundaries or saying no to themselves is also not good.

Our communities are riddled with incidents of road rage, entitlement conflicts, drive-by shootings and random acts of violence, all indicators that today's culture is spinning out of control along the same path that Noah saw in his day. Everyone wants to do as they will, but we are harming others in the process and doing so at alarming rates. We have become a society that demands from others yet refuses to surrender or offer anything of themselves. Relationship in community requires reciprocity, compromise and sometimes sacrifice – all enemies of the feel good addict.

Our world is living out Darwin's survival of the fittest. Churches have been subtly manipulated and some even forced to compromise their biblical truths in the name of tolerance and political correctness to ease the discomfort of others' choices.

In a world where everything goes, where everything is permissible, nothing is beneficial and no one is free except the ones who shout the loudest. The feel good addiction has become insatiable. Everything we seek for the moment to feed this addiction, will never be enough.

From the beginning of creation and all throughout history and into the present day, we have been groomed to self-destruct by an invisible enemy. The goal is to take us down and seduce us to take as many others as possible with us.

Biblically speaking, we've known this all along. It speaks of the devil roaming around, seeking whom he may devour. Starting with the deception in the beginning, and throughout the Bible, his methods are deceptive but his purpose is clear: to steal, kill and destroy mankind under the guise of providing satisfaction to what feels good to us in the moment. From a biblical perspective, I'd say the enemy, the devil, has been pretty successful.

Before you think this is all about the bible, we are about to unpack this notion of the feel good origins from scientific and psychological perspectives in the next chapter. While I am of the Christian faith, I also feel it is important to look at this destructive and deceptive ideal from all perspectives. Emotionally, physically and spiritually, this insatiable drive for self-serving mindset is woven intricately at the core of our DNA.

The feel good addiction is steeped in instant gratification and self-centeredness. It is impossible for it to not affect others' lives, as we have seen. Today, substance abuse, obesity (and its effects) and suicide are the top takers of lives. As I write this chapter, a new social media game among teens has emerged. The blue whale. A 21-year-old Russian man says he thinks of his victims as 'biological waste' and told police that they were 'happy to die' and that he was 'cleansing society'. The lethal game "involves brainwashing vulnerable teenagers over a period of 50 days, urging them to complete tasks from watching horror movies to waking at strange hours, and self-harming."[6] The real culprit behind this tragic ruse is one man not being able to deny his feel good addict.

We are a world made up of communities of individuals. We need to live harmoniously together, in love, care, respect and support if we are to survive. When one part of the whole only considers itself and others follow likewise, how can anyone feel safe much less live free?

Confession: *My father died in 2011. The death certificate says it was from colon cancer, diabetes and kidney failure. He really died from living his life the way he wanted to regardless of who it affected. Drinking himself to death. He was telling me one day that his drinking wasn't hurting anyone. I wanted so badly to say, "Really? Then why does your*

---

[6] http://www.dailymail.co.uk/news/article-4491294/Blue-Whale-game-mastermind-says-s-cleansing-society.html

wife have to bathe you, feed you, and help you on the toilet as a result of your drinking?" I could have spent hours recapping the countless fist fights he started, and the emotional and physical harm he caused our family while under the influence of his not-hurting-anyone feel good addiction.

If I knew then what I know now, perhaps I could have had a greater influence or impact with my father. Maybe I could have made a difference. The truth may have really made him angry, or it may equally have set him free. Something I will never know.

Change can only happen after we become aware of something that needs changing. Awareness is the first place to start, and that will be covered in the next chapter.

Is has been written and lectured that there is no such thing anymore as moral absolutes - and that is stated with absolute conviction by the creators of that concept! Throughout history, we have tried to undo absolutes, especially biblical ones as they seem to create the greatest negative response for the feel good addict. Societal absolutes make allowances in the opposite direction. The feel good addiction depends on having no limits and having no absolutes. This way of thinking and living has been reinforced through our development, taught in education, and celebrated in our culture. It is in our very nature, originating from the beginning of time.

Hopefully by now, you have seen the undercurrent of deception in our mini historical journey. "If it feels good, do it" has become the normal mantra of Western culture and increasingly influencing itself beyond the borders. The drive to feel good is at pandemic proportions across the globe and with an ever-increasing and unquenchable thirst for greater ways to be fulfilled as fast as possible. Much like traditional addictions, it has a voracious appetite and will stop at nothing as long as it has free reign to 'do as it wilt', in our lives.

We will talk in more detail in the subsequent chapters about addiction and how we can reel in this rampant phenomenon and affect change not only in our own lives, but in our world. We will also learn how to create a positive paying-it-forward kind of movement, but first let's begin with ourselves.

Before you move onto the next chapter and explore why we do what we do, spend a moment to take a snapshot of where you are at mentally, emotionally, physically and spiritually. Be honest with yourself and include why you bought this book. You are the only person who will see your writings. Burn them if you want afterward, but I encourage you not to. There can be a strong sense of accomplishment if you put what you write in an envelope and date it. And when you are finished reading this book, you can open it and see what insights you have gained, what attitudes have changed, and how much you have grown.

Here are a few questions to help you get started:

1. In what ways do you see a feel good addict active in your life today?

2. How do you think or feel your feel good addiction affects others?

3. What would you like to see changed in your life for the positive

Why We Do What We Do

Now for the big question. Why? Why do we have this inherent drive to seek pleasure and comfort, often forsaking all common sense or even life threatening consequences? We saw in the previous chapter how this started, biblically speaking, and how it has evolved. But beyond the bible, are there other complementary explanations? What motivates us and causes us to stay comfortable (even in misery), and why do we seek out more and more pleasure without seemingly any control over it?

It was touched on briefly at the end of the last chapter stating simply it is because we have learned to be this way. A feel good addiction is a learned and subconsciously programmed way of living. The historical and biblical origins of the feel good phenomena are compelling. Now, let's look at the scientific and psychological origins (with as minimal technical speak as possible!).

I think science is fascinating. As a behavioral science major, I love studying why we do what we do, and the things that influence our behavior. I am kind of a junky (no pun on the book title) of sorts when it comes to needing to understand things. The most fascinating thing of all to me however, is the intricate and complicated design of our bodies.

Several years ago I saw The Bodies exhibit at our local science center. It included a lit-up detailed look at our nervous system. It was absolutely fascinating! Did you know that our nervous system is made up of 100 billion to 1 trillion neurons or nerve cells communicating every moment of our lives? Or that our brains alone have around 85 billion nerve cells? To try to fathom that, here is a word picture for you: the human brain has more neurons lighting up in our head than the stars in the Milky Way!

Each of these neurons communicates using rapid fire signals across things called synapses (they do this without touching), fueled by chemically-charged transmitters. It's so crazy to think all that activity is going on inside our brains at speeds faster than any computer in the world. Simply amazing!

OK, humor me a bit longer for one tiny trip back to science class. Let's talk neurons. They are an electrically excitable cell that processes and transmits information through electrical and chemical signals. When we feel good, the experience stimulates neurotransmitting chemicals throughout our brain and body. Our pleasure chemicals—dopamine and endorphins being the main two chemical signal transmitters—are released.

CBS News reported that Neuroscientist Professor Gregory Berns from Emory University was intrigued (as am I) by the strange phenomenon of pleasure-seeking and the brain. Berns indicated that while pleasure is an instantaneous feeling of something good, why we seek those feelings is rather complicated. It is not just about our visceral sensations (feelings), it "is as much about our brains as it is our experiences." [7] What that means is that when we are driven to feel good, it's not just experiencing the actual 'feel good' that

---

[7] http://www.cbsnews.com/news/the-science-behind-pleasure-seeking-25-09-2011/

motivates us. It is rather about what that feel good *means* to us. Whether we realize it or not, we assign meaning to sensations and experiences and store them for future retrieval. That is how we learn. We touch fire, it hurts, so we avoid it. We eat sweets, it tastes good, firing off feel good signals, and we want more. Our neurons are always firing and training us in our responses and reactions. When we don't challenge those stored responses and consciously evaluate them, they can form patterns of responding that may or may not benefit us in the future.

The feel good things (and much of anything) we experience become rooted in our beliefs about them. If that caused you to stop and process a minute, don't feel alone, it did for me too. It is a pretty deep concept. So let's work it out together. When we seek to bring comfort or pleasure, it is not about the thing itself, but rather about what we believe about the thing. If we believe that ice cream will make us feel better, then it will. That creates a groove for us to follow. Consequently, every time we want to feel better, we will go for the ice cream. The same is true for things that have a negative impact. For example, when I was a child I had this beautiful copper cup that a man who hung out where my mom worked gave me. I drank everything out of it. One day I was drinking my favorite grape Kool-Aid and not being able to finish it all, I put it in the refrigerator overnight. The next day, taking it out and drinking it, I recall it tasted funny, but kept drinking anyway. Within minutes I was throwing up. My mom began frantically screaming on the phone to someone, then yelling at my brother to go get some milk.

I apparently was poisoned by the copper. It turned out the cup was not treated for drinking but was decorative, and in sitting overnight, the metal permeated my grape Kool-Aid, poisoning it. What followed was horrific. Neutralizing the poison was done with a half-gallon of milk and self-induced vomiting. I was about five years old at the time and to this day, I will not eat or drink anything that is fake grape flavored. I also have a high sensitivity to metallic and iron tastes and avoid anything made of copper.

Our brains and memories are powerful. They have a network of neurons responsible for noting discomfort and pleasure. Like my aversion to grape anything, so is our draw to things that bring pleasure. The studies in the past focused mostly on a defense than an offense. Meaning we spent more time looking at what we needed to avoid versus what we could move toward. "For much of the Twentieth century, scientists viewed pleasure as a second-class sensation, a kind of afterthought to the real motivators: pain and discomfort."[8] In the field of behaviorism, something called the theory of drive reduction basically forces animals to act to alleviate discomfort.

Behavioral scientist James Olds, who pioneered pleasure research in the 1950's, thought this was a dismal way to view existence, and many others agreed. This was because it completely dismissed the healthy, pleasurable things in life - Only recently has pleasure begun to get its due but it is turning out to be more complicated than anyone suspected.[8]

Kent Berridge, a neuroscientist at the University of Michigan, began working on the pleasure problem in the 1980s. Scientists at that point thought that dopamine, the powerful neurotransmitter associated with movement and motivation,

---

[8]http://www.slate.com/articles/health_and_science/science/2015/01/scie nce_of_pleasure_food_and_drink_ stimulate_the_brain.html

was the brain's pleasure chemical. But Berridge grew suspicious when, in an experiment with rats that had been given a dopamine suppressant, they still licked their lips when drinking sugar water, basically it is the rodent equivalent of a spontaneous smile. If rats were smiling without dopamine, he thought something else had to be involved. After years of experimentation, Berridge isolated what he believed to be a pleasure circuit in the brains of rodents, which was a conglomerate of knotted neurons near the brainstem, in which he dubbed "hedonic hot spots." When firing, they generate intense pleasure. Hedonic comes from the word hedonism which means the pursuit of pleasure and sensual self-indulgence.

The hot spots responded to several internal opioids, or endorphins. These are the brain chemicals known for their role in stress relief. Dopamine meanwhile in Berridge's view, is what generates the wanting, or craving. Both the craving and the pleasure response come from deep in the brain, stored in our instinct and reflex. For example, the enjoyment of sugar, food, or just about anything we find pleasure in, is the foundation of our basic behavioral cycle. Pleasure helps mold the brain's responses for future action. When pleasure responses get out of whack, they can be very hard to correct. This is what addiction is all about. Our brain becomes subconsciously molded for certain behaviors based on the level of pleasure and the meaning we assign to it.

This behavioral cycle is where we can be easily deceived. Our belief about a feel good sensation or experience is a crafty seduction that catches us unaware and wires our thinking to form patterns that cause us to seek it over and over again even throwing caution to the wind. Addiction is not just *substance dependence* (e.g. drug or alcohol addiction) or a *behavioral addiction* (like gambling or sex). It is anything a person does that is fueled by a strong urge that is difficult to control or give up. The feel good addict is reluctant to stop pleasure behaviors even if it means it will cost them their life. It is because *taking away pleasure means taking away meaning.*

Confession: *I have a weakness. I love cinnamon rolls covered in maple frosting. One day I was craving one real bad. I had decided they were off-limits for weight and sugar reasons, and I had not had one in months. But the battle was real. Everything seemed to smell like maple, even the rain! My donut synapses were firing off and the craving kept getting worse. I fought it off for what seemed like weeks, but the more I fought, the more I wanted one. It started with a simple casual internal suggestion of "I think I need to go to the store." Translation: "I need to go get a donut." I fight it, but lose. I wander through the store as if I am casing the place for a heist before I 'happen' to arrive in the bakery section. To my 'feigned' relief they didn't have what I wanted. As I started to walk away (with slight disappointment), the bakery manager asks if she can help me. Even though I say no, she must have felt my lack of conviction because she grabbed a cinnamon roll, took my arm and walked 'us' over to the bakery counter to see if they could put maple frosting on it. When they weren't able to, she marched me back over to the bakery case and handed me a giant maple bar. Told me it was on the house. A few short minutes later, alone in my care with the donut, I ate.*

When I came out of my donut stupor on the drive home, I was wondering what had just happened. This is where the mental games to maintain the pattern of addiction come into play. It struck me that I had been feeling stressed. I had a lot going on and became busier than was comfortable. I was often too tired to cook and eating poorly affected my sleep. The more sleep and healthy food deprived I became, the more I veered away from healthy patterns of coping, and the more the craving increased.

The meaning I assigned to this delectable little ditty of calories was from years gone by. As a teenager my bff and I would buy a couple of maple bars on lazy summer afternoons and eat them, laughing and carefree. The cinnamon roll was associated with calmer times at home as a child, smelling cinnamon rolls baking that my brother and I used to make. What I was really seeking was order, peace and contentment. It was the meaning I had subconsciously assigned to the cinnamon maple donut for years. The awareness of that was mind and life freeing (not to mention waistline limiting!)

While I was in my extreme craving, (trolling the bakery cabinet and eating the donut), I had no reflective or presently aware thoughts as to why. So, how did that happen? How is it that I consumed something without having any real conscious awareness of it until afterwards? Simply, I was programmed for it. I had done and played this pattern of responding to stress so many times before that it had created a 'normal' groove of responding. It was etched into my internal wiring.

Every story we hear about how individuals get hooked into and addiction starts with either one intentional or inadvertent engagement of the activity. Then it escalates until they can't stop thinking about it and begin creating bigger and better ways to get more of it. Food, alcohol, drugs and sex release the most powerful chemical responses in our body, which is why those carry the biggest impact to our world in the form of addictive behavior.

We cannot however dismiss the power of our subconscious. If you have ever been driving and all of the sudden you have no idea how you got somewhere, this is what I am talking about. A noise, a drastic change in environment (like your exit about to come up) will snap you out of your stupor. The radio gets turned down, you sit up straight and get your bearings. It is 'you' getting consciously present. Before that, your subconscious was driving without your conscious involvement. It takes over for things that we repetitively do that don't require active thought. Things we learn then file away as a pattern of movement and operation. Things like riding a bike, brushing our teeth and yes, driving a car. The first time you do any of those things, you are concentrating on everything you have to do. Checking your mirrors, or your hand position on the wheel. After time, they become habitual and we can do them without actively thinking about them.

If you're like me, you may have at one time or another, gone through the motions of turning your head side-to-side to prepare to pull out in traffic, and yet at the last minute, see a car coming. If you think about it, you were probably lost in a thought, yet your body did the motion anyway. The subconscious programming took over. Each subsequent time you do an action or behavior, it becomes encoded in your wiring so you don't have to think about each task being performed—like being on autopilot. The scientific world calls this dissociation (in a mild form). It's where you are literally mentally disconnected from the present. It is a mild form of what it's like when a person goes into shock. You are lost in the milky way of neural stimulus. You can still function, but consciously you are not fully aware until something snaps you out of it. A noise, someone saying your name, a horn or an abrupt change in the environment or patterns that are encoded in our psyche.

Confession: I had a former roommate who was an intense television watcher. I was talking to her one day, and even though she was responding with "uh huh" and nodding, she was not present. I thought it would be a great time to have a little fun. I said, "The office caught fire today, and some man attacked me in the parking garage." She responded the same way - 'uh huh'. A few seconds later she said, "Wait, what?"

Although her body and mouth were responding to me, there was absolutely no conscious processing of information until the information I was speaking didn't fit the patterns of typical information in her 'auto pilot.' I know many people who listen that way. It's actually cheap entertainment!

The greater the feel good sensations from past experiences, combined with a belief that the 'thing' will provide a sense of emotional and mental well-being, the greater the strength of the subconscious pull toward it. That is the power of addiction.

The association with maple cinnamon donut dating back to carefree times as a child was in the subconscious filing cabinet, just waiting for the right combination of scenarios to be retrieved. Once we are aware, when a craving comes, we can do a check internally and do something different to bring in a more beneficially appropriate response, something with less addictive values. Like breathing, getting present and centered.

I had a therapist tell me years ago that when I feel like whatever I am going through is reaching a point that I won't be able to endure or function any longer, she said just stop and breathe. Then, wait fifteen minutes, and see how things look. That was an amazing, life-changing tip. It gets you out of your head and into the reality of the present.

Carl Jung, a Swiss psychiatrist and psychoanalyst who founded analytical psychology, captured it so well when he said "until you make the unconscious conscious, it will direct your life and you will call it fate." The feel good addict's subconscious mind often works against the betterment of their well-being. Once patterned, it affects how the brain works in processing information. The thing that brings us the most pleasure will dominate our thinking until we bring it into our awareness and give it conscious evaluation. If we do not bring ourselves to become aware, one harmless pleasurable experience can become subconsciously compulsive, interfering with even ordinary responsibilities such as work, relationships, our health, and even our lives.

I found an interesting parallel between science and the biblical accounts that we tapped into during the last chapter. Science says we are driven to satisfy the feel good because of what that experience, sensation, or satisfaction means to us. We assign meaning to things and it creates a specific level of chemical response. The greater the meaning, the more intense the response. In the biblical account, Eve first saw that the apple was nice looking. She then 'believed' what the serpent said when he told her it was not only good looking, it was also good tasting and she would receive something pretty significant. It was her belief in what the apple would give her that was her deciding factor, not about the fruit itself. What we want is never about the thing itself. It is about what it means to us.

From the combined viewpoints, biblically, scientifically and psychologically, it feels safe to say that what happened in the garden, set the tone for how we think, believe and behave. The apple truly didn't fall far from the tree.

The subsequent chapters will capture how being a feel good addict plays out in every area of our lives and how we can begin to make the 'unconscious conscious' and overcome the destructive impact it has on our lives and the lives of others. We will unpack how we assign meaning that has a deceptive twist that keeps us stuck in the comfort zone, living the status quo and settling for good enough.

Before you move on, you may find it helpful to get the most of this section by taking a few moments to reflect on these questions.

1. What are the 'feel goods' that are in your life? (Ex: substance, food, coffee, chocolate, busyness, excessive exercise, etc.)

2. When do they increase in need to be fulfilled? In other words, when do you feel you need them more than at other times? (Ex: during stress, tired, happy, sad, etc.)

3. On a scale of 1-10, how often do you try to fool yourself like I did with the donut? 1 being rarely 10 being always.

4. Are any of your feel good items listed in question 1 affecting how your feel about yourself?

5. Are any of your feel goods affecting others around you?

Our Health

We have one body and one life here on earth. How we take care of ourselves mind, body and soul, (or not) determines not only the quality of life but longevity. What this and the following two chapters will cover is how the feel good addict affects us individually in our health, wealth, and career, or sense of purpose. It is here that we see it making the dominant and sometimes relentless demands on us. It is here that we will find ourselves compromising in small ways that can evolve into bigger ways, consequently spilling over into other areas of our lives and the lives of others.

Since our health is what keeps us alive (and without being alive, the feel good addict would be a moot point!), it seemed fitting to start there. Each year, nearly 900,000 Americans die prematurely from five leading causes of death: heart disease, cancers, chronic respiratory illnesses, stroke, and unintentional injuries. Yet, according to a study from the Centers for Disease Control and Prevention, twenty to forty percent of the deaths from each cause could be prevented.[9]

The feel good addict is something we must face in every decision and choice we make every minute of the day. In our exceedingly fast-paced microwave world, it takes more effort to think things through all the way to their consequence before we act. Our culture, the media and even schools encourage this

---

[9] https://www.cdc.gov/media/releases/2014/p0501-preventable-deaths.html

fast-paced lifestyle. We are encouraged to lean on technology more and more. In school, students do math with calculators instead of working it out in their heads or on paper. Wall clocks are all digital so learning to tell time has been replaced with being told the time. I will never forget when I told an employee to come and see me at a quarter to the hour, he looked at me puzzled and said, "What time is that"? I said fifteen minutes before the hour. Still, he could not understand what I said. Then the light bulb went on. "Oh," he said, "45 after." When I asked him why he saw it that way, he said that is how the clocks at school show it - 7:45.

Don't get me wrong, I love technology and moving fast. My favorite thing to do is project management. The fast moving of many parts. On top of that, I was in Information Technology for the dot com world. What concerns me and what has challenged me about the feel good addict is that when we ride the wave of constant moving and shaking, we don't think about the little things in our lives that have monumental effects. Like our health.

The simple things such as how much water we drink. Years ago I did a study about dehydration and was shocked to discover that at least seventy five percent of most Americans are dehydrated on a daily basis. Since our bodies are made up of between fifty five and sixty five percent water, consuming the right amount of water is quite important. When we are dehydrated, our blood becomes thick and increases the pressure in our arteries, which can cause the heart to fail or the body to produce blood clots. It also prevents our blood from adequately carrying the necessary oxygen throughout our body. The heart and brain are comprised of seventy three percent water. Irregular heartbeats, flutters and skipping can many times be settled into normal rhythms by just drinking water (magnesium deficiency is also a culprit for irregular heartbeats as a side note).

Our brains alone are made up of approximately eighty five percent water and depends on having abundant access to this life giving fluid to keep our moods stable, energy up and anxiety down.[10] Water is a free anti-anxiety, anti-depressant beverage with no side effects, except good health. It has been experienced by many, including myself that headaches, sad and depressed feelings and agitation can easily dissolve with the consumption of this prescription free medication called water. The rule of thumb for the average activity level person is to drink half your body weight in ounces per day to keep you adequately hydrated. If we don't supply our bodies with enough water, we aren't able to flush out toxins from the air and our foods and keep our muscles and nervous system functioning properly.

I have heard hundreds of people say they don't care for the taste of plain water. Water is virtually tasteless. The real truth is that we are more accustomed to the added chemicals and flavorings that most drinks have, making water taste flat and tasteless. Coffee, alcoholic drinks, soda and other sugary or synthetic drinks don't add water to our system; they actually *take away* our water supply due to the chemicals or diuretic properties of many of these beverages. The body needs water. Pure and simple water. Without it, we die, albeit a slow death.

---

[10] http://today.uconn.edu/2012/02/even-mild-dehydration-can-alter-mood/

Another argument I have heard about starting a water drinking regimen is that it makes you go to the bathroom too much. The best indicator if you have been walking around dehydrated is how much you pee when you start drinking more water. If you give yourself a few days, you will find that the frequency becomes longer in between. This is because our organs and muscles begin absorbing it the way they are supposed to. In the beginning it is like everything is a dried out sponge. When you pour water on a hard dry sponge the water just rolls off at first. Then slowly the sponge becomes softer and more water begins to absorb. Our bodies are the same way.

If water is something you aren't fond of at the moment, try adding lemon or a drop of honey into your water or having non-chemically altered sparkling water until your taste buds acquire the taste for water. If you are a carbonated water drinker, in spite of some studies saying it harms your blood, studies have shown that it is indeed safe to drink. It can however exacerbate the symptoms of some digestive problems.[11]

The bottom line is that, if you can associate the good the water is doing to your body versus the taste you seek, the meaning of it will help satisfy and shut down the feel good addict to satisfy the fake tastes you have gotten used to. Your body will thank you!

The feel good addict in us also has a way of transforming slow affecting illnesses into life-threatening and life-taking diseases. Things such as obesity, alcoholism, preventable diabetes and unintentional injuries due to inadequate physical

---

[11] http://www.livestrong.com/article/313171-health-risks-of-carbonated-water/

fitness are all causes of illnesses that can generally be avoided. I shared in the previous chapter a small part of the story about my father. He died at 71 from preventable consequences of alcohol abuse. It was a slow, progressive death that had a great deal of effect on those around him. I remember when he found out that his aortic valve needed to be replaced due to the effects of his drinking. The doctor told him that he needed to stop. He did for a few months and until shortly after the surgery. He told me that now that he had a new pig valve for his aorta, he could go back to drinking. Within a year, the onset of peripheral neuropathy began. It's where you start losing feeling in your extremities and it is quite painful. He also was having severe gout in his feet, another painful consequence. When the onset of type 2 diabetes emerged, it inspired him to stop drinking beer. He switched to the hard stuff. The next progression was he started getting sores on his legs that wouldn't heal, his skin tone was ashen and his legs were too painful to walk and were shiny and bright red. Within a year, he was no longer able to help himself on or off the toilet or in and out of the shower. He was only 65 when he hit that level. One day he fell inside the shower, cutting his leg badly on the shower rail and hitting his head. His wife couldn't help him up. He laid there bleeding badly, yelling at her to not call the ambulance but demanded to get a neighbor instead. His blood was so thinned because of the alcohol it wouldn't coagulate. His wife told me later she feared he would bleed to death in the shower as she watched helplessly.

It was after this incident that he finally stopped drinking. It was too late to reverse the neuropathy and the diabetes. Within a few short years he was put on dialysis. His oxygen levels were depleted from his compressed marrow from years of alcohol abuse that limited the production of his oxygen carrying red blood cells, so he always felt winded. Not too long after that, he had a leg amputated. On June 14, 2011, only a few months past his 71st birthday, he went in to have a routine stint added to help the dialysis flow better. When he was being released, he complained about having difficulty breathing but the nurses and his wife told him that he was fine as that was not unusual for him. They wheeled him out to the car, sat him the passenger seat and he mentioned again that he couldn't catch his breath. His wife sat him back and put his seat belt on. Milliseconds later he slumped over, took three rapid breaths, and was gone. In the parking lot of a hospital, unable to be saved by anyone, my father died from a preventable disease.

Why do I tell you that story? Because his feel good addict is what killed him. If you recall in the previous chapter, I had asked him when he was going to stop drinking and he said why, it wasn't hurting anyone. The feel good addict can be deceptive. It actually hurt him mortally and, hurt those around him more than his death did. The sad thing for me is seeing others following that same deceptive path, brushing it off, justifying that it is their way of having fun and ignoring all the signs that say the body feels otherwise. Some say it is heredity and can't be helped. That is only partially true—we all are stricken with the feel good addiction in our internal wiring but it is something we can re-wire if we want to. Our feel good addict wants us to stay where we are: comfortable. Even if it kills us.

Confession: *I started drinking chai lattes from a chain coffee shop in 2002 after being introduced to them by a friend. By the end of 2003, I was up to an average of three 20oz frothy beverages per day. The hook for me was not the flavor but the feeling it gave me. They resembled a hug in a cup or a pat on the back. It provided a sense of comfort and reward. I have* *battled this off and on for 15 years. In the first few years of drinking them, the large quantities of milk that made up the latte (I wasn't a milk drinker) caused me to become lactose intolerant. So I switched to soy milk. After another year, my skin tone started to look ashen and I appeared to have aged in years. Then weight started piling on and I was constantly bloated. I would 'try' to stop by drinking a different beverage, but the pull was too great. When I began having pain behind my stomach that presented similar to pancreatitis, it scared me enough to stop. (The fear of a serious illness was greater than the pleasure). Eventually, the pain subsided into a faint memory. Again, I ventured back into the addiction.*

This back and forth addiction still continues as I write this (just in case you wondered if I had it all figured out). This drink was the main instrument in me putting on about 60 extra pounds of weight. As a result of this book, I decided to face the meaning behind the drink. Much like the story of the donut, it was about happier times. When a friend introduced me to fluffy coffee drinks (of which I was only a straight coffee drinker) it was a social event. There was laughter, good conversation, smiles, encouragements and just pure easy-going friendship. When I began buying more and more of them it was during a time when I was about to leave for Russia for three months. When I returned, all hell broke loose. Drastic changes in my career, ministry and a close friend was dying of cancer. No wonder I wanted the calm cool and collective easy days of friendship feeling back. Because in reality those days were past, the chai (much like any other substance) became my friend, companion and warm fuzzy.

Breaking these patterns of relating to a substance with meaning is not easy, but doable. It requires first being aware. Second, evaluating the situation and finding an alternative that is lesser in its addictive pull (sugar is a powerful substance, greater than cocaine) or unhealthy.

After that awareness the pull has become less and less and easier to say no to. The longer a pattern of behavior is present, the more up front work has to be done to lick it and form new grooves in how we see and respond to life. As I was thinking about a person I know and my father, it struck me that I am on the same path, only a different choice of beverage. That reality hit me pretty hard.

I am not saying that alcohol or sugary coffee drinks in and of themselves are bad. It is the excess consumption and the combination of other contents that cause unhealthy effects. For instance, the large quantities of milk I was consuming in the lattes was more than my body could process. When I switched to soy, I was unaware that I had an allergy to it and as a result it was slowly shutting down my immune system. These are things we don't think about until we are sick. We end up overeating, choosing foods and drinks that satisfy something other than what is needed. We need water, we need nutrients, and we need to eat balanced from real food.

What our feel good addict wants is opposite to what our body and mind needs. There is nothing wrong in eating and drinking things that have very little nutritional value, but as a replacement or in excess, it is slow suicide by food and beverage consumption. Stopping, thinking and asking ourselves why we want something (and getting beyond the canned answer of "because I want it") will help us to not fall victim to this self-destroying part of this addiction. There is a verse in the Bible that came to mind as I wrote this: "Everything is permissible, but not everything is beneficial". [12] That certainly captures the feel good addict perfectly. It also resonates and causes me to pause and think. I hope it encourages you to pause too.

In one of my many careers, I was a massage therapist. I learned a great deal more about muscles than I ever knew as an athlete. Our bodies are similar to suspension bridges. Our muscles are the cables and our skeleton is the driving deck. If one cable is off, it will throw the whole rest of the structure out of whack, and it will be lopsided and unable to function the way it was designed. Many years ago I had severe sciatica that was unbearable. I could find no relief from the nerve pain on my skin or in the numbness in my leg. I went to physical therapy where I was told I had a dislocated hip and two bulging lumbar disks. Weeks of therapy gave minimal results. I was sent to an alternative type of therapy that used giant magnets for half a fortune, requiring extensive and expensive non-insured repeated treatments that did nothing. As a last resort and out of desperation, I made an appointment with a massage therapist (before I became one – no way was someone going to touch me). In two visits, the sciatica was gone. She told me that she had released a small muscle that was connected to another muscle, which was the one that was compressing the nerve channel and pulling on my low back and hip. Because of that one tight muscle affecting the others muscles, it presented as if I had a bulging disk and a dislocated hip. When that muscle let go, everything righted itself. What an amazing suspension bridge our muscles are!

---

[12] 1Corinthians 10:23

I tell that story because every spring and summer, emergency rooms are filled to the brim with couch potato athletes. Between 2011 and 2014, 8.6 million people went to the ER for sports related injuries. Television sets are turned on for more than a third of the day— in fact about eight hours and 14 minutes a day! There are usually more TVs than people occupying a home. The reason people are hurt from preventable injures is because we have in many ways stopped caring for our bodies. We choose to eat poorly, move less, watch TV more and then blame it on aging.

Confession: *I was a pretty good athlete in high school and then again in my adult life. In school I was a varsity track sprinter and I ran for a major company's corporate track team after I graduated. I tried basketball once in junior high, but didn't make the team. Although I could outrun anyone to the other end of the court, I couldn't shoot, much less dribble. In my late 20s I took up soccer and softball. My rabbit sprinter reflexes were a great fit as a goalie and center fielder in fast pitch. During my soccer career I acquired a few broken ribs, a bruised cheek, and a torn rotator cuff. In softball I only experienced torn knee meniscus. I wasn't a home run hitter, but I was a consistent base hitter out of the infield and a pretty good base stealer. In 1994, I managed to qualify to participate in the US Olympic Teams women's fast pitch softball tryouts.*

Fast forward 20 years and I am on the field with men and women playing slow pitch softball. My cleats were stiff, my mitt needed oil badly, and my ball bag smelled like an antique store…not to mention I was 50 pounds heavier and very out of shape! I hadn't sprinted in years, much less jogged, and I had a previous hamstring injury that still bothered me from time to time. (Why is it when we get older that we think we can pick up where we left off as a fit younger person?). The game was only 10 minutes in and it was my first up to bat. I lined up, saw the pitch and nailed it over the second baseman. Bam! I still had it I thought. As I dropped the bat and planted to run, my leg collapsed and down I went. The OTHER hamstring epic fail. I picked myself up as casually as I could and somehow managed to still make it to first base before the fielder brought the ball in. As I crossed the base bag however, I tripped and fell face down.

There I lay with a 12" long bleeding dirt rash on my non-just-injured-hamstring leg. I wanted to do nothing more than crawl under that base bag and hide. The look on my teams face was: 'she is an Olympic level athlete?' Yeah... not that day.

I was the epitome of a middle-aged athletic has-been. Yes, in case you were wondering, I had to be carried off the field. If that wasn't bad enough, with me out, my team would have to forfeit if I couldn't get back on the field. When it was our turn to be back on the field, they asked if I could at least pitch. I hobbled out there with all the heroic ego-saving strength I could muster. The first batter hit a line drive right at my head. Thankfully, those track instincts kicked in and I was able to duck in time to save my head, but unfortunately not my hamstring. I went down in a screaming pile of flesh, fighting the vomit rising in my throat and the complete mind-blackening embarrassment I was feeling. There was no going back on the field that day, or since.

My injury wasn't because of age. It was because of a failure to maintain flexibility and strength in my muscles and fitness levels. I had a friend recently tell me that the reason we are overweight and can't seem to lose it is because we are older. I asked her how then are there thin old people?

I do know it is a bit harder to get those extra pounds off as we age, but it's not so much that we are older, it's that we move less and eat more of the foods we shouldn't. Why? Because it takes more thought and effort to exercise and cook. As we age, the driving forces to impress others isn't so important. We stop caring as much about what we look like and accept all of our imperfections and give into the total satisfaction of feeding our feel good addict. The psychological and politically correct media reinforces that mindset. It encourages us to love our chubby little bodies and couch potato lifestyles as a celebrated way of life of 'just being ourselves.' I have to say, "Really?" We may be ourselves, but not our best version. It's similar to saying, "Congratulations, you are cutting years off your life!"

Obesity can definitely affect how we feel about ourselves. We are taught that obesity is okay in the name of acceptance. While we do need to love the whole person of who we are, loving blindly and carelessly is not healthy. Obesity has been found to change the dopamine receptors in the brain which are responsible for motivation. Obesity causes them to decline, creating a vicious cycle for the feel good addict that includes failing to exercise, increased cravings for sugary and carbohydrate-filled foods, and basic inactivity in general. The results? More and more weight gain, followed by sickness and disease. Obesity can creep up on us over time. We can be fit and healthy as we move into middle age and then suddenly, one day we wake up overweight and wonder how that happened (or is that only me that thought that?). Unfortunately, it doesn't happen overnight, and it doesn't leave that way either. It is a slow process of making good choices every day and delaying the feel good addict until it no longer has power. I still thought I was a fit athlete. In my mind I was, but definitely not in my body.

According to health standards, I was obese. I didn't feel like working out, exercising or being as diligent about my fitness as I used to be. I, if I am to be honest, was not interested. It wasn't all that important to me anymore because, in my mind, I couldn't find the 'why' for why I should exercise and eat healthy. I associated the meaning of fitness to performance rewards (or getting attention). I used to be a finely-tuned machine. I needed to be that for the sports I played. No sports, no tuning. I also liked the self-satisfaction (another feel good), of the accolades, trophies, medals and ribbons I got from my ability, but in the off-season, it had no strength to keep me motivated.

Confession: *In high school in between track season I could be found smoking out by the 'rock' in the school yard, and partying on the weekends. In season, I was obsessively disciplined. Out of season without my performance and attention feel good rewards, I had no motivation.*

I find it to be very important to find inner motivators or else consistency becomes as fickle and fleeting as emotions. Motivators like health, longevity and not having to keep upsizing clothes can be great inspirations.

The bottom line is our whole body is connected. When one thing is out of balance—emotionally, mentally or physically—it affects the whole of who we are. Diet, exercise, and care for our bodies—these things are not meant to torture, deprive or punish us from enjoyment or pleasure. They are meant to give us a lifetime of enjoyment and a long-lasting life of breathing for many more years to come.

When David Shaw said the pleasure police are taking away everyone's fun I think it is more like they are trying to save their life. Whether it is cinnamon maple donuts, ice cream, pie, cake, chocolate, sex, gambling, performance, perfectionism, workaholism, exercis-ism, or my nemesis, chai tea lattes, too much or too little of the right or wrong thing will shorten not only years off our life, but it will impact the quality of it as well. Everything is permissible, but not everything is beneficial. Our lives are more important than any fleeting momentary pleasure of whatever our thing or things are. We don't have to stay stuck in the vicious cycle that the feel good addict wreaks on our body. There is a way out. When trying to improve our health, we must first stop the preoccupation with diets and food management as our default setting. Diet alone did not shape a world class athlete, and our nation's obsession with eating (in the name of diets) will not solve the obesity crisis. If you are determined to break the cycle of your feel good addict, you will need to develop a lifestyle that affects positive change and that will excite, motivate, and kick-start you into new habits to sustain a new and healthy lifestyle.

The Center for Disease Control recommends an activity level of at least 5 miles a day in movement. That's about 10,000 steps with a fitness monitor. Prevention Magazine wrote an article for 15 ways to get 10,000 steps in a day without going to the gym. The link is in the footnotes.[13] You can also start any one of the myriad exercise plans found on-line for free, or join a local gym. Next step would be to start adopting a good balanced eating plan, including enjoying in moderation the things you can't and don't want to live without. One that I have found that works wonders for many is the 80/20 rule for eating, the details for which can be found on-line. If you are a

---

[13] http://www.prevention.com/fitness/15-ways-to-get-10000-steps-a-day-without-exercising-more

diabetic, you can explore the Ketogenic eating plans that are physician-endorsed and are making incredible strides getting type two diabetics completely off medication. Search the Internet for both of those and find not only the foods to help you stay healthy, but thousands of recipes to keep it exciting. Your feel good addict will find a new thing to embrace. Good health - because you are worth it.

Questions for reflection

1. What areas in your health do you feel out of balance?

2. Think of three things that can motivate you to take care of yourself.

3. Of those three, which is most important?

4. Now that you have motivation, list three action steps you will take and when.

Our Finances

Statistically speaking, nearly half of all American households don't save any money. Americans spend more on shoes, jewelry, and watches ($100 billion) than on higher education. As a country, we consume twice as many material goods today as we did fifty years ago and shopping malls outnumber high schools. Ninety Three percent of teenage girls rank shopping as their favorite pastime, and the average woman will spend more than eight years of their average lifespan shopping in some form or another. Americans overall spend $1.2 trillion annually on nonessential goods, and nine out of every ten American rent an off-site storage facility in the over 50,000 plus storage facilities in the United States. In comparison, that is more than five times the number of Starbucks coffee shops. The remaining percent of Americans spend $8 billion dollars a year on home organization materials.

The United States is a wealthy nation, yet many live in poverty and extreme debt. This chapter will expose the reality of how the feel good addiction has robbed many of a life of contentment and freedom from debt.

In 2005, three of the major television shopping networks combined shipped over 193 million packages to households in the United States. We know by now that the feel good addiction is what drives this need to satisfy any desire we have with abandoned restraint, regardless whether we can pay for it or not. Consistently choosing immediate reward over delayed gratification is the power behind the spending aspect of the feel good addiction. Those who seek instant gratification have a now focus. They are also less able to control impulses and are more susceptible to temptation because they have great difficulty becoming aware of what is driving the impulse. It truly is an 'if it feels good, do it' mode of operation and the feel good addict does not want to wait.

Delayed gratification on the other hand says 'wait, let's think this through.' It's the awareness factor that needs to truly come into full on focus in order to bridle the feel good addict.

In a book called *The Modern Social Conflict: The Politics of Liberty*, author Ralf Dahrendorf states that the "ethic of saving, hard work and deferred gratification, which had dominated centuries of capitalist economy growth" in the past has "at last succumbed to a culture of immediate enjoyment."[14] He went on to say that in the 1980s, "although saving was the classical engine of economic growth in the past, it was replaced by credit." The average individual American has just under $17,000 in credit card debt alone. A delayed gratification mindset of 'work now, save and spend later' has been replaced by 'spend now, work for it later, and forget about saving.' In fact, nearly half of American households don't save any money.

We can be honest, we like being comfortable. We don't want to miss out on having pleasures at our fingertips. We want our boats, cars, houses, garages, marinas and neighborhoods filled with our possessions in the event we want to go play or have a good time.

---

[14] Dahrendorf, Ralf - Transaction Publishers; 2 edition, pg 137 (September 24, 2007) ISBN-10: 0765803852

In 2002 I went to Russia for a mission trip. In preparation they strongly recommended that we bring pictures of our home town, families and things that are special to us, but to absolutely refrain from pictures and possessions that display wealth. They also strictly asked us to not talk about income. The reason is that most Russians, (the poor and the twenty percent middle class that exists today), have only a fraction of the possessions that Americans have, (and that we don't use). They live out of necessity, much like they eat, and we live out of want. I'm not innocent. I have owned fast cars, multiple cars, a big house, water toys and motorcycles amongst the 'stuff' I just had to have. After being in Russia and living in a twelve by twelve room for three months, coming home to my big house felt so odd. Today, I live in a hugely scaled down modest home, small yard, one car and have only inline skates and a bicycle for toys. This is not saying possessions are bad. But, to have so many that are used maybe one time a year if that, is something to consider before opening up our wallets.

In truth, the feel good addict can't get enough 'stuff,' and they can't wait to get it! I was astounded in my research for this book to discover that the average home has over 300,000 items in them. That is pure craziness. Home sizes also have tripled in size over the past fifty years.[15] Present day new construction neighborhoods are so jammed together to fit the biggest houses possible, there is often less than twelve feet between the next house. It is like giant apartments with a fence between instead of walls. What that means is no one goes outside anymore to entertain. Yards are being replaced by fences and barbeques are cook and go back inside events instead of linger and enjoy, just

---

[15] http://www.becomingminimalist.com/clutter-stats/

so people can get some privacy. Consequently, to avoid the discomfort of feeling invaded by peering neighbors, the average American will sit inside, either watching television or playing video games instead of engaging in relationship through conversation.

In 2015 it was reported that sixty five percent of homes owned some form of video game-playing device and spent around $23.5 billion dollars on gaming media.[16] If we are not watching television or playing video games in our homes we go out and pay to do it in larger venues. In 2012, $25.4 billion dollars was spent attending sporting events, $8 billion in sporting apparel and $54 billion on food. When we put all this in visible perspective, is it any wonder we don't have any money to save.

Historically, we saw that we are really programmed for the quick, the fun and sometimes, irresponsible. Sadly, we carry this mindset from generation to generation. The average ten year-old owns two hundred and thirty eight toys, but usually only plays with just twelve. And when they get older, they become like us: spending and buying things we either don't need, will use maybe once or never. Things we think we can't live without. If only we would fill our lives and homes with things more meaningful, like relationships, life might have a bit more color and peace.

Do you want it all now, or are you prepared to wait? Michelle Obama unwittingly caused a national French debate over working on Sundays. It seems the First Lady wanted to

---

[16] https://www.polygon.com/2016/4/29/11539102/gaming-stats-2016-esa-essential-facts

take Sasha and Malia shopping while they were there. The only problem was that stores were not open on Sundays. Prime Minister Nicolas Sarkozy personally called a few stores and asked them to open and has since introduced a law to allow shops in touristy areas to remain open on Sundays. A spokesman for the Communist Party responded, saying Sarkozy had "crossed the line." Clearly, Michelle Obama, like many of us in the United States, had been living a feel good addict lifestyle and was unconscious of how different life is when delayed gratification suppresses the feel good addict. Like not working on Sundays!

The feel good addict has a focus on the right now. To really begin to overcome this addiction in the area of finances, a solid close look at personal responsibility is the key to overcoming and living debt free.

When I was a child, it was no big deal to plan dinner. My mother would ask me to put the potatoes in the oven for dinner at a specified time to allow for coordination of the other items being cooked. Potatoes usually took forty five minutes to an hour to bake. After about thirty minutes, the house would begin to smell wonderful as they baked and the other things were being prepared. The anticipation of the flavors that would soon be ready was like having Thanksgiving every day. Today, it is often hard to ascertain what is cooking underneath that plastic covered container holding our three minute and thirty second microwave meal.

I remember in school watching science fiction shows depicting the future where eating a pill could be a complete meal or absorbing the contents of a book. In more recent movies such as a popular franchise where children are sent into an arena to kill one another as a form of a entertainment to the city dwellers, there is a scene where the winners from previous years are at a party watching everyone eat until they are sick. When trays of more food is passed around, the children decline stating they are full. The city dwellers encourage them to drink a pink liquid intended to make them vomit. The reason they gave was so they could keep on eating and not miss out on so many flavors and choices.

We want everything now. Even waiting one minute for water to boil is becoming an irritation for many. I was in the grocery store the other day and every checkout stand was long and seemed like they weren't moving. A father and his daughter were behind me and the little girl kept asking why they didn't move to another line that seemed to be shorter to her. He said it was because they had too many things in their baskets and it would take longer. That was a teachable moment.

Delayed gratification is a thing of the past. If we want something to eat, we go to the store, restaurant or fast food shop and get what we want in just a few minutes. No effort or labor. No real planning or thinking. We want it and we go get it, regardless if we can afford it or not.

Confession: *I was about to redo my backyard last summer and I wanted to bring in some extra dirt. I did not own a vehicle capable of carrying a load like what I needed, nor did I have trailer. In the spirit of the feel good addict, I began looking online for trailers immediately. I wanted to take care of my dilemma now. I was moments away from putting an offer on one I found when I was suddenly struck by a thought: When I'm done hauling the dirt, what will I use it for? Where will I store it? It was those questions that forced my programmed brain wanting to 'do it now' to get present. I realized I didn't need to buy a trailer. It was like coming out of a fog. After a few more moments of thought, I ordered dirt to* *be delivered. I saved myself a few thousand dollars and space in my driveway.*

I think it is so interesting how when it comes to life in general, we live and think of the future or our pasts but rarely in the present now. When it comes to spending money, we actually only live in the immediate moment, the now, without really being present. Such a dichotomy! We function in a mode of autopilot directed by our inner feel good addict. We have minimal conscious reflection of past actions or future consequences when this is the mode of thinking. If we take just a quick moment to stop our movement, think, reflect then make a sound decision, we all might be a little wealthier, have less debt, more space to move around in our homes and a considerable reduction in stress.

If you are buried in debt, or have a hard time saying no to impulsive spending, don't lose heart. Start small. Set boundaries for yourself. When you see that shiny object or the great deal you don't think you can pass up, freeze. Stop and take a breath. Walk away, do something different, do anything so you can have time to actually visualize seeing that thing in your house, on your body, or wherever it will end up as soon as you buy it. Project out in your thoughts a month, or six months, even a year from now, and see if the thing still matters. If not, pass it up. It will be a bit uncomfortable at first, but with practice, you will be successful.

Questions for reflection

1. What things have you purchased in the last year that you had to have, but no longer use?

2. What things have you purchased that were impulsive and you regretted?

3. What commitment to yourself will you make to practice delayed gratification as it pertains to spending by thinking through before you purchase?

4. In thinking about waiting to buy something until you have the funds, how does that make you feel inside?

5. If you are in debt more than 10 thousand dollars, what steps will you take to begin paying it down?

Suggestions: Financial Peace University with Dave Ramsey[17] and an article on 10 steps to Financial Freedom.[18]

---

[17] www.daveramsey.com

[18] http://www.lifeway.com/Article/10-steps-to-financial-freedom

Career and Purpose

I used to work for an aircraft manufacturing company years ago. Although I started in the factory, by the time I quit, I was working in an office. There was a guy in our work group who every day did the same routine. The first forty five minutes of his shift, he would wander into everyone's cubicle and start a conversation about nothing in particular. We all determined that even though he was a nice enough guy, he just didn't care much for working.

In those forty five minutes of his every day he was stealing time and money from the company and attempting to invite others to engage with him in his poor work ethic. That is not an uncommon occurrence. Many companies and organizations all over the world experience cubicle profit thieves like this. Years later as a director of Information Technology for a startup dot com, I was amazed at the reasons employees would come up with for why they weren't working. Things like, 'I'm researching.' Translation: 'I'm surfing the Internet.' One of my favorites was 'I was helping someone log in.' (with their feet on the desk, kicked back and laughing... for two hours?).

Hey, I get it. Some days we just don't feel like doing what we are being paid to do. Some days we just want to ride the time. This chapter will have two sections within it covering how the feel good addict shows up in our workplace and in settles for good enough, affects others and even sacrifices our dreams for the safety of the comfort zone.

I can bet there's not one person reading this right now that hasn't taken at least one office supply from work in the up to current lifetime. It was probably not done intentionally either, at least the first time. I've done it with pens, pencils, paper clips, binder clips—heck, I've even made copies of software. That was pretty intentional! Don't judge me. It was the early 90s and no one thought anything about it, especially to think it was piracy!

That is one of the things about the feel good addict that can really get us in trouble: maniplication. It's a new word I created just for this book. It means "manipulating" unconsciously and creating a "justification" consciously to make it seem right. As I mentioned in a previous chapter, the feel good addict's patterns and grooves have a way of getting stuck in our subconscious.

The first time that we take a pen, we may say "Whoops!" to ourselves when we discover it in our computer case, pocket or purse. If we don't return it, which many of us don't, over time we discover we like how it writes. One day we discover the ink runs out. So what do we do? Honestly, many of us will intentionally take another one. No whoops, no absent mindedness. We plan and execute a well thought out pen stealing caper. The feel good addict will convince us that it is not stealing (manipulation). It's ours as part of being employed at our company (justification).

Confession: *When I was in my twenties working at a major airplane manufacturing company, at just 5'2" and barely over a hundred pounds, I was selected to be what was called 'a wing rat.' I spent my days crawling inside and inspecting airplane wings. Over time, as is typical in a company like this, you end up moving around to different shops depending on staffing needs and your specialties. Eventually I ended up working in* *the final assembly line. As a quality inspector, I had to be there at 3:00am often to oversee the aircraft body parts joining to one another. The first time watching the cranes move these huge metal tubes into place to join with the rest of the airplane body was fascinating. But every seven days, which was our cycle, it became like deja vu. My role during this process was to make sure the gaps between the sections being joined were within Federal Aviation tolerances. Any overage could cause drag in flight or offset the ability to handle the aircraft in inclement weather. If we had a good body join load, then we would have a great deal of time to kill before our normal shift started. On occasion, when we finished early, instead of seeking out a supervisor to volunteer for something to do, I would often go over to the wing area, climb inside, and take a snooze. That might sound innocent, but I was still on the clock. I too was stealing from my company like my former co-worker.*

The first time I slept in the wings, I was terrified and barely slept because I was worried I was going to oversleep and miss the regular shift start. As time went on, it got easier and I got more creative. The feel-good addict teaches us how to compromise our values and principles for the sake of our own comfort.

If we are an employee, no matter what level on the chain of command, unless we own the company we have a responsibility to keep our feel good addict in check. Our employer has no other obligation to us except to pay our wages. No one is entitled to anything more than that and any other mandated requirements by local, state or government authorities. If an employer offers anything more, it's not an entitlement, it's a gift and blessing. That may sound harsh to some of you reading this, or you may think your circumstances are different. I hear you, but please know this: the feel good addict doesn't give up comfort that easy. I've worked for great companies and awful companies. I've had bosses laugh in my face and fire me when I turned in my two week notice. I had an employer manipulate me to agree that I was quitting so they wouldn't have to pay me unemployment. I have also had executive directors cry with me when I resigned. I have experienced life as an employee and an employer. Ironically, many things that I did as an employee inadvertently and some intentionally, came back around to me.

The second area for this chapter that is near and dear to me is where I think our feel good addict shows up the most. In a failure to live out our purpose or calling in life. If there is any place the comfort zone is most active, it is here. According to Forbes Magazine in 1987, sixty one percent said they were happy with their jobs. In 2014, only forty eight percent of Americans were satisfied with their current job.[19] What changed? Simply, people lost interest in their work.

Did you know that the average attention span for a goldfish is nine seconds? According to a study conducted by Microsoft,[20] people generally lose concentration after eight seconds, one second less than a goldfish! The study highlighted the effects of an increasingly digitalized lifestyle on the brain—or a brain that is programmed for instant gratification and pressed for more and more stimulus. As we seek new and creative ways to activate our feel good chemicals, we become less and less satisfied.

---

[19] https://www.forbes.com/sites/susanadams/2014/06/20/most-americans-are-unhappy-at-work/#341a1e17341a

[20] http://time.com/3858309/attention-spans-goldfish

When we live a life flowing out of our purpose, it can shut down the feel good addict and lift us out of the comfort zone faster than anything. It is a calling forth of the fullness of our true self. There is nothing more powerful to overcome the shiny object syndrome than the mind and heart of a person living, breathing, and doing what they were created to do. It is a strong presence that pulls out from the very core of our being and is capable of pulling us out of the deepest pit of complacency and distraction. When we know our purpose we find a new sense of focus, self-leadership and motivation. It deactivates our feel good addict quickly.

An example of that is boredom. When we are bored we may sit in front of the television, eat or sleep. I don't know about you but when I am bored, I feel like a slug. The only way that shifts if I find something that fires me up and excites me. Not a feel good excitement but a productive accomplishing something excitement. I love creating curriculum, journalistic videos and writing. When I get going on a project in these areas I have to set an alarm to remind myself to eat. Those are things I am passionate about and fit me to a tee within my purpose. When I am not doing what is in alignment I can easily get distracted and bored. Discovering what our purpose and passions are is a powerful way to step out of the comfort zone and live your life on purpose.

Many employees in all types of organizations experience feelings of being trapped or in a rut. If more employers helped their employees discover how their purpose and calling fits within the framework of their company's mission, they would not only weed out those who are not a good fit (square peg in a round hole) or those who are planning to be short timers. In addition they would strengthen the workforce of those who are the right fit but maybe in the wrong role. Increases in productivity and profits not to mention morale will be greatly and positively affected.

As a member of the John Maxwell Team, I learned about leadership from the best of the best in the world. In everything John teaches it always comes down to this quote from Zig Ziglar: "Give people what they want and they will give you what you want."

———————————————

Do you know why you are here? Do you know what you want in life? What you really, really want? I was asked that in a workshop one day. What I discovered were the things that set my soul on fire and changed my life. It is not about finding the right job title or role that you try to fit yourself into. It is about that 'thing' you do when you are just being you, at your best and then going out and doing it. It may be with a company or something you create yourself. Think about it....

- When you are at your best, what are you doing?

- Who are you with?

- Where are you physically in that moment?

- What in that moment is most important to you?

I realized during that workshop that what I learned was something I needed to share with the world. I decided to get trained and licensed to teach it. For more about this workshop or for interest in the online course, go to my website at www.micheleALewis.com.

As I was attending this workshop what came out for me was that although I enjoyed the contract job I was doing, day-by-day I felt it chipping away at my real purpose for why I was alive.

It was as if every day something was sucking the life right out of me. In just a few weeks after the workshop, I resigned from that contract job. Today, I feel alive! I am writing, speaking, coaching and inspiring others to never settle for less than who they were designed to be – professionally, personally and spiritually. Doing that including writing this book - THAT is who I was meant to be!

Other things have changed since that day as well. An awakening of sorts happened. I literally felt like new life was poured into me. I began doing a much better job at taking care of my body and making sound financial decisions. Every day, my resolve strengthens. There is a lightness to my step, and more days than not, I get out of bed with excitement to face the day.

"If one advances confidently in the direction of his (or her) dreams, and endeavors to live the life which he (or she) has imagined, he (or she) will meet with a success unexpected in common hours." Henry David Thoreau

That quote speaks volumes. I believe that the key to overcoming the power of the feel good addiction is to discover why you exist. What and who you were meant to be. What you are good at does not necessarily mean that is what you were meant to do. Your purpose in life will never change. It is what you are compelled to do, and it will show up no matter where you are and no matter who you are with.

Confession: *Just a few years out of high school, I began working at the aircraft company. Fourteen years later, by a series of being at the right place and the right time, I landed a position with an international insurance brokerage as a systems manager. My role was flying around the country, implementing technology in a traditional paper and pen world, and developing training for fifty two field offices. I was in my element running complex projects with ease and efficiency. I was good at! Within two years, I was promoted to assistant vice president and became the Pacific Northwest Region Automation Account Executive. I reported directly to the top – the Director of Information Technology at the company's corporate headquarters in Chicago. Overnight it seemed that I went from blue collar manufacturing to white collar corporate, hobnobbing with CEOs, CFOs, and anyone else with an O after their name! I felt that I had arrived. I was doing something important and I felt important. Not because of I was doing what I loved, but because I felt important and was very successful.*

There were many downsides once the status and oh so important ego lost its luster. The first one that made me weary was I only spent a week at home every month. The rest of the time I was on the road, in the air or in a hotel. My life revolved around keeping the CEOs apprised of corporate initiatives and keeping corporate apprised of the mischief the CEOs were up to. (That's how it began to feel anyway). On a flight to Chicago almost three years into the job, I was stuck on a tarmac in Denver for hours waiting for a lightning storm to pass. This was an international flight, heading to Germany after Chicago. As I sat there feeling frustrated, I found myself tuning in to a man behind me talking with an elderly couple. He was a missionary to Poland and Germany and he began sharing a story about how he and his team would visit a warehouse a few times a year. It was in East Germany, and it housed Christian items confiscated during uprisings over many years and decades. In my mind, I was picturing this huge never-ending warehouse, but no doubt probably was not that big. The missionary shared how each time they went to this warehouse over a period of a few years, they would see the same guard in front of the doors and would strike up a conversation, often sharing the gospel to him. The guard always seemed expressionless. Sometime prior to this man being on this plane, he and his team went to the warehouse, but this time, they found the door open and the guard nowhere in sight. They went in, calling for him, but there was no answer. In the distance they thought they heard what sounded like weeping, but could not quite make it out. As they continued to walk, following the sound, they eventually found this guard. A man who was usually stoic, expressionless and unbending, sat on the floor of the warehouse, holding a bible and weeping. The missionary team slowly approached him and just sat with him. Eventually the sobs subsided. With tears still running down his face, he handed the missionary the Bible that was in his hand. It had belonged to his grandparents.

That story is forever etched in my memory as the most profound defining moment of my life. How was it possible that a lost Bible from decades ago, buried deep in the recesses of a huge warehouse found its way into the hands of the only living family member two generations after being confiscated? It was nothing short of miraculous.

As I sat in my seat on that plane trying not to let anyone see me crying, I felt God speak to me so loudly the answer to what I had been asking Him inside for months. Was this all I was meant to do? His answer was positively a great big NO. By a powerful supernatural force, I knew in that moment that I was created to do something that, for me, had a deeper meaning. I enjoyed my job and was good at it, but I knew that I was created to make a difference in lives. In the bible there is a story about a conversation with Jesus and the apostle Peter. When Jesus called Peter to follow Him, Jesus said come and I will make you a fisher of men instead of fish. That is what it felt like for me. I was helping people streamline their work and learn to collaborate with each other. Jesus was about to shake my world and teach me how to help people simplify their lives and bring meaning although at that time I had no idea I would be where I am today. All I knew is that moment that Jesus was calling me deeper in and higher up and until I stepped outside of my comfort zone and dared to risk the known for the unknown, I would never discover the so much more that was awaiting me. When I arrived in Chicago, I submitted my resignation and the director and I hugged and cried.

My feel good addict didn't have a chance or a say in that moment. Since that day, now 23 years ago, God has taken me on many adventures of trusting Him as He unpacked and revealed the details surrounding my purpose in life. This book, my friends, is one expression of that. My words for you are: don't settle for the comfort zone or status quo. Life in that space is empty, dark and lonely. Don't let your feel good addict keep you from living a life that is just 'good enough'. You are created for so much more.

Take some time to sit alone, without distractions, and ask yourself the questions I listed in the middle of this chapter. You will be pleasantly surprised what may unfold for you! Don't wait until you are at the end of your days to discover the real you. YOU are waiting to break free!

When you discover your purpose it may not be to leave your job. It may not be to start your own business. But I can guarantee it will be revealing, illuminating and life changing.

When you discover the real you and begin to explore what you were meant for, it will set your soul on fire! You are never too old, never too young, and it's never too late to be all you were meant to be. Go for it!

Relationships

Friendship is vital to our overall well-being, but in today's social media frenzy, we can become so easily satisfied with a few likes and superficial comments on our posts, and call it relationship. The feel good addict is just fine with their one thousand 'friends', (and if we are honest, many we have no idea who they are or how they connected with us). This chapter will explore the impact the feel good addict has on our ability to have meaningful relationships and how it impacts our emotional health.

According to research done by Dr. Robin Dunbar, an evolutionary psychologist at the University of Oxford, the maximum amount of relationships we can mentally manage is about one hundred and fifty.[21] Within that group however, Dunbar says it's the closest fifteen relationships, including our family members, that matter most. Even though our family might be the ones that will be there for us when we need help, Dunbar says it's our good friends that will bring on the satisfying experiences in our lives. He says they actually will help us release feel good endorphins. Those are the same feel good feelings we get when we exercise. Dunbar goes on to say that the "vital friendships—the pals you hug and laugh and lament with—are the ones who have the greatest impact on your health and happiness." His research indicates that for optimal well-being, the healthy number of friends we need in our lives is between three and five close friends.

---

[21] http://time.com/3748090/friends-social-health/

This I found to be an interesting counter to the feel good addiction. In the first part of this book we looked at how neuro chemicals give us the feel good feelings. But we also saw that it is about the meaning we assign to the feel good we are experiencing. If we consider friendship, the good friends and experiences we have with them being able to illicit good feelings, then why does the average person today have so few real meaningful relationships? I believe the feel good addict convinces us to substitute them for things that are easier, quicker, have minimal commitment, and are less messy.

The onset of social media has created huge gaps in real relationships and more and more people live isolated lives every day, even if their social media says they have thousands of friends. We are designed for relationships and will fail to thrive without them. In 2015, "according to data from the General Social Survey (GSS), the number of Americans who say they have no close friends has roughly tripled in recent decades. "Zero" is also the most common response when people are asked how many confidants they have, the GSS data showed. Adult men seem to be especially bad at keeping and cultivating friendships.[22]

We need relationships to keep our health in balance. When we are laughing with our pal, or feeling him or her touch our shoulder in sympathy, the resulting rush of endorphins seems to "tune" up our immune system, which Dr. Dunbar says can help protect us from disease.[23] Those are the healthy feel goods for the feel good addict. Dr. Mark Vernon, a philosopher,

---

[22] http://time.com/3748090/friends-social-health/

[23] http://time.com/3748090/friends-social-health/

psychotherapist and author of *The Meaning of Friendship*, says that "for the sake of your health, you need friends—ideally the really close kind you see face-to-face on a regular basis. But even one very good friend can improve your life in profound ways."[24]

Relationships can be messy. But they can also be amazing! Relationship is defined as a state of being connected. The definition of connected is to 'join together so as to provide access and communication.' When we take two people with different personalities, different ideas, values, principles beliefs, and yes, baggage, and we somehow manage to click and enjoy one another, that is relationship.

With relationship also comes conflict, misunderstanding and hurt. Sometimes the feel good addict can ruin a good relationship when they become a little messy. Most of us are really awesome when our relationships are smooth, comfortable, easy going and complimentary. But what happens when things get a little bumpy, not so easy and downright messy? In the spirit of the feel good addict, many will simply respond with 'I don't need this' and bail. There is a difference between unhealthy and healthy relationships. I am not talking about toxic people, abusive or otherwise dysfunctional on the extreme end. I am referring to the healthy normal aspects of differences of opinion, reactions to stress, hurt, and the things that create challenges in our relationships.

It is so important to be aware when our feel good addict creeps in so we can get a handle on it before disaster strikes and destroyed relationships occur. One of the biggest ways I have

---

[24] http://time.com/3748090/friends-social-health/

witnessed (in others and myself) a few ways the feel good addict shows up in our relationships is in our expectations. If we are being honest, there are plenty of times we would love to have (or have had) an adult temper tantrum when things don't go our way – either inwardly or outwardly. If we're not careful, we can become THEY people. You know, the 'they' never call us, 'they' don't say nice things to us as much as 'they' should, 'they' never do what we want to do, 'they' are insensitive, and 'they' only want us when 'they' don't have anything else to do. They, they, they. So often "they" are quite possibly thinking the same about you.

Confession: *I have a person that is currently in my life that I have known since I was ten years old. She rarely calls and almost never asks me to do things with her. She has however been faithful for the past twenty five plus years to send me a birthday card every year. We currently live about ten minutes from each other but sadly she has only seen my doorstep once. It's not that the invitation hasn't been extended but it seems to never work out. When we were in junior high I had asked her to go to the movies with me and her answer was: "Sure, if something else doesn't come up." The moral of this story is that even though we are not BFFs by definition, she is someone that I value and I know she values me. The hardest place I had to get to was to accept her for who she is and what she is willing and able to contribute in our friendship. What she does or doesn't do with or for me does not have anything to do with what I can contribute to the relationship. For her, extending a birthday card is good. For me it is time just hanging out. The compromise is I go to her when I want to be 'her' friend and in turn get my friend fix.*

Friendship is as much giving as it is receiving. When we begin to create a score card for who does what and when, that's not relationship. That's control and manipulation. The feel good addict likes to keep score. A sort of tit for tat relationship style. Holding on to an offense is the best way to destroy any relationship. There may have been times my friend was hurt because I was not consistent with sending her birthday cards. She has never said as much nor have I pressed her for not calling or coming over. Over the years we have come to negotiate the relationship and adjust expectations. That's how longevity and quality are created in relationships.

Every relationship takes work and intentional effort. Sometimes they are not fifty-fifty. Sometimes they are one hundred to zero, and sometimes they go back and forth in between. That is life, friendship and relationships. They will get messy. They will have ups and downs, and ebbs and flows. When our feel good addict starts to demand the other party in our relationships be one hundred percent 'on' at all times to meet us in our expectations, they slowly become toxic and erode the foundation. This in particular is seen prominent within family circles. Henry Cloud, author of Boundaries, one of my favorite cut to the chase writers and speakers, captured this topic perfectly as it pertains to our relationships as adults with parents. Even though you "feel like you always have to honor your parents, you don't always have to obey them. If you're still in the child position, then that is getting in the way of how you were meant to live your life". Relationships are a privilege, not an entitlement. That is true between parents and adult children.

One of the best dressed up manipulative feel good addict attitudes I see over and over on social media is the variations of the saying: 'Real friends can go months without ever talking, because they know their friendship resides in the heart.' I think that quote should just be honest with what that really means: 'Although we say we are friends, it's really one of convenience.' Real friends may not have to talk every day, but they certainly need to connect regularly to keep the connection alive, fresh and healthy.

I hear many people say they don't know what happened with a friendship, especially with a long-time friend. Heart felt wondering of how they fell away when they were once so close. When asked what they think happened, it is usually followed by the other person stopped responding or distance and time created a chasm. I have said those exact same words and dismissed it as 'it is what it is'. When I got inquisitive and really asked myself what could have happened, it was revealing. My feel good addict merely waited for the other person to reach out or I gave up after a few attempts. There seems to be some magical number of times that we determine is good enough before we stop trying to stay connected. The feel good addict will assume it's about the other person giving up or no longer interested. Often the feel good addict will wait, and wait...and wait for the other person to step up. Friendship requires intention and action.

The real key with relationships is not whether they are important. Many important relationships die. It's about whether 'we,' our each individual addict, is more important than the friendship. The feel good addict will always lean toward self-satisfaction, convenience and ease. A friend takes as many steps as possible, even out of their own comfort zone, to invest in the relationship. If it dies a natural death after much effort (emphasis on MUCH), then there is not much that can be done. At least you will know that your efforts were intentional and genuine.

Another reason the feel good addict will give up too soon on a gone stale relationship is because instant gratification doesn't occur. Sadly both parties may miss out on an amazing relationship. The feel good addict doesn't like to hear, life happens. A friend might be having a rough time and doesn't know how to talk about it just yet. Maybe technology snafus have caused difficulties. If both parties put aside their feel good addict's self-centered expectations and think of the other more than themselves, many broken friendships and relationships quite possibly could be avoided. Ralph Waldo Emerson captured relationships best in this quote that calls out our feel good addict: "The only way to have a friend is to be one."

There is a huge difference between friends and acquaintances. In our fast-paced world, we have become accustomed to quick information instead of deep discussion. Everywhere we go we find more and more people with heads buried in tech devices. Emoji's are used instead of a real smile, and cryptic texts sent at a rapid fire pace replace phone calls and in person conversations. As a result, we tend to gravitate towards other things to get that feel good fix—spending, substance abuse, and out of control behaviors to name a few. Imagine a world where our friendships were pursued with the same priority we put on our purchases and eating? Now that's an amazing vision!

The get to the core truth, we can't be a friend or have a friend without ever seeing, talking, or engaging with each other regularly. We need to connect with intention. It doesn't matter what catchy little quotes say about good friends not needing to see each other regularly. Life happens way too fast for large chunks of time and touch to come in-between.

If we want to have good, healthy relationships, we need to get honest and make the time and effort to invest in those people we want to keep in our lives. If we have people that make us feel 'healthy' and happy even when things get messy, then those are the friendships we need to cultivate on a regular basis. Make a date to get together, and keep it. If it is long distance, make plans to speak or video chat. Try to make an honest effort to at least once a year, connect with your distant relationships in person. Albert Einstein said, "I fear the day that technology will surpass our human interaction." I fear that that day has come.

Confession: After living in a community for nineteen years, I moved to be closer to my family. It was only seventy five miles away, but it felt like it was across the state. I had many relationships in my town and it was hard to leave. But out of the many relationships, one has stood the test of distance. This friend was very instrumental as I journeyed through the difficulties of life. I was also able to be there for her when her life difficulties occurred. Once I moved, this friend feared that we would disconnect as we were no longer down the road from one another. But distance is not something unfamiliar to me. My family has not lived near me in years, and some are in other states. I assured my friend that we would not lose touch. I was committed to holding my end of the friendship up. This was because I had experienced the same promise when I was a teenager. My best friend moved one summer while I was away camping with family. When I returned home, she was gone. We wrote each other for the rest of that year, but the letters got to be fewer each month that passed. When a month turned into several months, my parents allowed me to make a long distance call. Her parents said she was grounded and could not talk on the phone. I never saw or spoke to her again. I was not about to let that happen with my current friend (I was pretty certain she wouldn't be grounded either). I have now been in my new location almost three years and my friend and I actually feel closer than when I lived nearer. We have become intentional in our relationship with calls, emails and in-person visiting. I know she will be my friend for life.

Whether its friends who are not as close, family or children who have moved out of the house, being intentional and committed to connecting and staying connected is essential to maintaining and building relationships. If you are going to pick up the phone, dial instead of texting. Make a point to do some face-to-face connecting, even if it is via technology. Reach out to that old friend you haven't spoken to in a while. Send a card or email to a family member. Let someone who is or has been important or special to you know that you care and make a point to keep it up. It is never too late to try to reconnect. Even if you find the relationships has suffered a permanent disconnect, not knowing is worse. Be the friend you want others to be to you.

Questions for reflection

1. Name the friends you once were close with that you no longer are connected with, try to find them and reach out.

2. What things have you done recently to let someone you care about know they are important to you? If nothing, why not and when will you?

3. When you are with someone, are you preoccupied with your phone, social media or television? If yes, make a plan to be all there when you are with them.

4. If you have a relationship that got messy and you miss that person, what steps will you take to reconcile?

Home and Pets

I live in quaint town in a small neighborhood community. It was quite the culture shock for me to be in such close proximity to people after being fairly isolated on two and a half forested acres for close to twenty years. Sounds of owls and coyotes were replaced with people sounds that I wasn't used to (or fond of). One sound that I found most heartbreaking was the sounds of a dog whimpering in the night, hoping and waiting for its owner to hear them and invite them in.

After living on acreage and only hearing sounds of nature, having a small yard and too close for privacy houses has been both a blessing and honestly, a pain. Being reduced to a small yard is a blessing in maintenance time, and having neighbors around in the event of something catastrophic is comforting. However, listening to conversations (no matter how hard I try not to) that are best left for the bedroom or tavern, that, I could do without.

After having conversations with neighbors and actually being close enough to make observations, I saw how the feel good addict affects us in this setting as well. What is interesting about this chapter is it reveals how our feel good addict impacts others outside the walls of our homes, ourselves in our homes, and with our furry companions. We are in community with our neighbors and our pets.

I live in a pretty nice neighborhood. I don't mean upscale, I mean a nice people neighborhood. Our houses are modest, clean and neat (for the most part). I had the opportunity to have a conversation with a next door neighbor who actually inspired me to write this chapter. This neighbor, a young husband, came out to talk to me one day as I was mowing my lawn. Our discussion began with him telling me how he was unable to mow his lawn because his puppy chewed the pull cord. He followed this statement with 'and he couldn't by a new lawn mower because his wife had the card he wanted to use to purchase one' (the lawn mower was chewed two weeks prior I discovered). We continued discussing his lawn mower dilemma and then moved on to my yard. He was envious of how my yard had been transformed by the work I had done and expressed desires to 'someday' do the same to his. It was that last statement that was immediately followed by 'but' that grabbed my literary attention. The 'but' was because he said he never seemed to have enough time plus he was too tired after work to do much of anything.

Now, this story needs to have some context. Here are a few observations that I have made over the past few years living here. This is the same guy who comes home from work every day and either loads his mountain bike in his truck and heads out to ride, has buddies over, or with great detail, washes his truck.

Our feel good addict is slippery. It convinces us that we don't have time for (or are too tired to do) the things we need to do, when in reality, we really just don't want to do them. My neighbor truly has the time and obviously is not too tired but rather is more interested and committed to his own feel good activities than his responsibilities. Where this feel good addiction crosses over and impacts others, namely his close neighbors is with the blackberries that are climbing the fence, the weeds in the median between our houses, the endless amount of kiddie trash that flits with the wind into my yard and the accumulating yard waste that is a rodent buffet.

His feel good addict affects myself, the other adjoining neighbor and the quality of our neighborhood. The good news is that his truck is clean and he is physically fit.

Confession: *As a child, I was burdened with the monotonous task of doing dishes every day. I am not talking about rinsing and putting them in the dishwasher. I'm talking about the old-fashioned wash and dry by hand doing of dishes. In addition, because we had no clothes dryer, I was tasked with hanging up the laundry either on a line in the basement or outside. To this day, I loathe laundry and dishes. What I noticed however is, that if I don't do these things, they do not get done. I live alone. I find that I will make up every excuse in my head to not do the dishes. I'm tired. It will take too long. I don't feel like it. While it is great that I have these choices now as an adult that I was not afforded as a child, it affects me differently if they are not done. It creates in me a feeling of disorder and chaos (not to mention no clean dishes to use). When I take the time to clean up after I use them, I feel somehow centered. There is order in my house. The same is true for the laundry. I get frustrated when I can't find any clothes, then realize the clean ones are still in the basket waiting for me to put away. I can go weeks plucking out of the basket, and I hate it every time I do it. Yet I don't change. When I get ready to get into the shower and discover that the last pair of clean undergarments was from yesterday's plucking, I then berate myself for not folding the laundry so I wouldn't be in this predicament.*

My problem is that I was seeing these tasks through the filter of the past and not the truth of the present. It is true that the filter through which we see our present circumstances can be skewed by our past experiences. However, like any other confrontation to our feel good addict, when we make the unconscious conscious, what we see takes on a whole new dimension. The subconscious can distort reality. The truth is that today's task of dishes and laundry (or whatever your avoidance task is) is not even remotely the same as the past. I stood over my sink reflecting on this, and instantly became aware that no one was telling me to do these dishes. I wasn't made to stand there and miss out on family time, because I live alone – I am my family! There weren't four others in the house that I had to clean up after, as there were when I was a child. I don't have a basement with bugs and rodents where I have to go and hang up the laundry. I have a dishwasher. I have a clothes dryer. This awareness of truth set me free. Next comes the repackaging for the present. If I did the dishes, which takes about five minutes, I thought about how that would make me feel? When the laundry basket is empty, and I open the dresser, I will know exactly how many days I have left before I run out of my unmentionables. Domestic Freedom!

It takes but a minute to get present and to undo years of feel good habit forming behavior we create to avoid something discomforting. I hated going into the basement with the rats climbing on the floor beams to hang up laundry. To this day I will not own a house with a basement. Perhaps my neighbor had experiences as a child where he was always tasked with chores and never fun play time with his friends? Think about that task you avoid like the plague and ask yourself what it reminds you of. Face it. Bring it into the present and create a new pathway for your own freedom and success.

The flip side of this is that procrastination or avoidance has nothing to do with our past experiences but rather present choices to simply avoid responsibility and keep our feel good addict completely satisfied. Regardless of what the motivating factors are, conscious awareness and responsible actions are something that needs to be addressed with our feel good addict. Take time to reflect how well you keep up your home and yard. What does it look like from your neighbor's perspective? Do you have plant growth that encroaches onto others property affecting their efforts to keep things contained? Is your litter and trash attracting unwanted critters that create much more than just a nuisance? While we all have different ideas and opinions of what looks good and nice, there is one thing we all have in common – we don't like it much when someone's expression of freedom to be sloppy, affects another's' freedom to be neat. If we want to let our feel good addict continue to run rampant in our neighborhoods maybe we could be kind by merely keeping the addict contained within the walls of our own homes and not allowing it to venture outside.

There is a paved trail in my neighborhood where I regularly walk or ride my bike. On one section, there is a house with a huge yard that has four dogs tied to chains on cables suspended from the trees. They can't get within fifteen feet of each other. There is no social play available to them and each dog has their own makeshift dog house to somewhat keep them out of the elements. I've walked by in the rain, snow and heat and these dogs are always outside. When people walk by, they bark. I have never seen a human around them. Never have seen them off their cables. Somedays I see them standing in the rain, just staring at the big world at the end of their chain.

For some, I think the idea or novelty of having a pet sounds great in the beginning, but when the newness wears off, it can turn to the drudgery of maintenance. Things the feel good addict will avoid at all costs. Recently I read how people lined up to relinquish their dog to the shelter after realizing they didn't want the responsibility of caring for them. Very sad.

Confession: *I have three pets. A dog and two cats. Some days I feel like all I do is pick up poo. Between all three, litter sifting, doggy poopy sacks and vacuuming pet hair can feel like a part-time job, but I love my pets. They are my companions. I knew what I was getting into when I got them. What I didn't count was the impact my newest addition, my dog, would affect me and impact me. I rescued a five year old German Shepherd that appeared to have had a traumatic background. I don't know all of his history but what I do know is he has anxiety and is uncomfortable around people taller than about four feet. I have had dogs all my life, and many of them were rescues. None of my experiences prepared me for this. It took two weeks for him to let me pet him. On our walks, he would jump at sewer grates, plastic bags, balloons and soda cans. If someone was walking behind us, he would incessantly look back to keep an eye on their whereabouts. When they passed us, he would slow down to create a wide berth. When I came time to go on a work trip, I panicked. What was I going to do? Who could I get to sit with him that he would allow to even let him outside? Should I give him back to the foster care family? All those questions swirled in my mind. Friends encouraged me to give him up. It would have been easier to just hand him back. Easier on me. But I made a commitment to the foster family, and this pooch. The poor pup had been with five different homes because no one had the patience for him. As much as this challenged me, I didn't want to be number six.*

Our feel good addict is notorious for giving up and giving in at the hint of difficulty or challenge. My pup definitely requires planning that has not been easy. This challenged me a great deal. No doubt, those who have special needs children or pets, can completely understand what I mean when I say the only option is adjust and get over yourself. It's not about *us*.

When I travel, whoever I get to sit with him also needs to be patient. They have to be willing to come over for visits at least two weeks in advance. Even then, it isn't always smooth. I have had him now for almost three years. He is not like other dogs, but he has improved. He now plays and follows me everywhere. I have a sitter for him that he adores and remembers every time she comes over. However, there are still small things that can send him backwards after months of improvement. Today, as I write this, he is hiding in the closet. The oven timer spooked him. Earlier it was someone closing the lid on their recycle bin that cut our walk short. He is on hyper-alert and it will take hours, if not days, for him to feel safe again. I don't have to go into detail for you to know how the fourth of July impacts him.

Pets are our companions and sometimes the only real family we have. Just as with our relationships, they take time, effort and intention to maintain, not only their daily rituals, but also their health and well-being. I am not going to go so far as to say we need to treat them as humans, they are after all, animals. But we do need to treat and care for them with respect and dignity. They trust and depend on us to do so.

Our feel good addict can also, like in relationships, keep us from being present with our pets and we can subconsciously treat them like house or yard ornaments. They can irritate and agitate us when they don't behave or damage things, (as is the case with one of my cats and my furniture). When we are busy or frustrated with something unrelated, we can also take it out on them. The way to successfully navigate and overthrow the pet-unfriendly feel good addict is to take a moment and get outside of ourselves and think about those furry friends (or scaly or feathery) and be thankful for their undying love and commitment to us.

Pets need attention, care, and, most of all, love and patience. If you have a pet that feels more like a burden than a joy, I encourage you to stop and look at them. Take their whole being into your senses. Look in their eyes. Watch them sleep. Look at the intricate markings. Listen to their purr or the quiet woofs of a puppy dream. Remember why you got them. In spite of all the animal shenanigans, you are the only thing that keeps them safe and alive. They depend on you. Enjoy the few short years you have with them and their unconditional love.

Whether you have a huge house or a small house, small or large pets, the feel good addict will distort the need to tend to our responsibilities and subconsciously turn them into annoying inconveniences. Fido needs you. Fluffy needs you. Your neighbors need you. *You* need you to be present. To be responsible. To sacrifice your feel good for the sake of those that depend on you and those you are in community with.

Questions for reflection:

1. How well do you tend to your house and your yard?

2. Take a moment and be your neighbor. What do you see and experience as you look at your home and activities?

3. What are your pet practices? Do you spend time with them and if no, what will you do about it?

4. In what ways are you neighborly?

Relationship with God

I wrote this chapter on Good Friday. The day that Christ was beaten, pummeled and bloodied, then hung on a cross for us. The same day my feel good addict was whining about wanting my nemesis chai latte. After a mild temper tantrum, I overcame the temptation to indulge where I eventually found myself reflecting on what Good Friday meant. I recalled that Christ cried tears of blood, pleading with the Father to take the soon to occur suffering from Him, yet he surrendered to the Father. What followed was his lonely and agonizing walk on the path to Calvary, where He died a painful death, giving up his life for all. It wasn't that his life was cut short by some cruel gesture from God. It was always destined to be so. That was why he was on the earth. That was his purpose. It was the only way for a corrupt world to be fully reconciled to a Holy God.

For those venturing into this chapter wondering what on earth I am talking about, or for the curious wondering how a bloodied depiction of a man dying on a cross has anything to do with being a feel good addict and being stuck in the comfort zone, well, I hope you will read on. It is because of what Christ did that the feel good addict has the most hope of overcoming the pitfalls of the comfort zone. Because of the cross we have access to supernatural strength and support.

There is a passage in the book of Isaiah that I think really captures the feel good addict in all of us and why we need something greater than ourselves to help us conquer the sometimes powerful urges of this addiction. I am going to break out the verses to simplify this concept. In verse six of chapter fifty three it says, "*We,* every one of us have strayed away like sheep! *We,* who left God's paths to follow our own." That is the plight of the feel good addict. Do as we wilt, or if it feels good, do it. As a result, God turned us over to do whatever we wanted. When He saw that we were hell-bent (pun intended) again to destroy ourselves, He planned a way for us to be reconciled back to Him in relationship. You see, when Adam and Eve broke relationship with God by saying, "Hey, we want to do things our way," the only way for mankind to be able to even remotely be in God's presence was to be purified, because He is Holy and pure. The only way that could occur was through a sacrifice of blood. Blood makes an atonement, or makes right what is injured or wrong, because there is life in it. The Red Cross, blood banks and every hospital in the world understands this. If someone is injured, has a disease that is killing them, blood that is taken from another is given to them in order to heal or save their life.

When God came to earth in the form of the man Jesus, He offered Himself as the blood donor for all in the world. Verse five of Isaiah fifty three says, "He was wounded and bruised for *our* sins. He was beaten that we might have peace; he was lashed, and we were healed!" The only catch is that mankind has to ask and receive His donation in order to get this life saving blood transfusion.

If you knew you were dying, and the only way to be saved was to have a blood transfusion, wouldn't you accept? You would go through the painstaking process of acknowledging you have a disease; one that is killing you, and ask to receive a lifesaving donation. The hospital would find a suitable donor and offer it to you. They would find one that is a perfect match and if you wanted to live, you would gratefully accept. What you didn't know is that because you needed so much blood, it would cost the donor his life. This is what baffled the doctors. Why would a donor give up his life for someone he didn't know? After the transfusion and recording the time of death for the donor, something miraculous happened. He came back to life, but was in a coma. For two days they waited for some indication he was coming out of it, but there was nothing. The morning of the third day, he woke up. Fully restored, and no signs of any damage. His blood saved your life and although he was dead, he is now alive.

How do you think you might respond? Would you be relieved or dismissive? I'm going to venture that you would be feeling beyond grateful. You might ask, what you could do to let him know how much you appreciate what he did. When you sit down and meet with him, you discover that he had one request. That you would stay connected to him. To talk and take time to learn about his life and to be mindful of how you care for your life from here on out. In addition, he told you that no matter what time of day, when you need a friend to talk to, or need help in anyway, come to him first, he will always be there for you. That sounded pretty easy compared to what he did for you. So you agreed. Then he said there was one more thing. If you forgot and became distracted to maintain the connection and be intentional about caring for your life that, over time, subtly you would become weak and sick again. It might not be noticeable at first, but one day it will hit you and you possibly could die before you realized how much distance had come between you.

The Cross of Christ is all about what God did for us by becoming human, as Jesus, and dying on the cross to redeem us from the folly of ourselves. Because Jesus was obedient to the death for you and me, God raised him from the dead to live forever. He said anyone who believes in His name and confesses (acknowledges) that this was done for them as a life-saving gift, they would receive the same gift and would be connected to God the Father, the Son Jesus and his Spirit for all eternity – alive and well! He only asks of us to walk closely with him.

As we have seen historically, when men and women, left to their own devices, create massive amounts of misery before dying and returning to dust. Like the life-saving transfusion, we are left with a choice. Our way and its consequences, or His way and life. Many sadly choose the latter. Or, like we saw with Noah and those after him, when the honeymoon of gratefulness passes, the old familiar feel good addict seeps in and the subtle deception of life as it once was begins slowly to take our life from us.

I think the Christian Life is one in which many have forgotten what it cost God for them to live. We are happy and satisfied with salvation and all the amazing blessings, but when things get tough or begin to stretch us, we aren't so eager to pick up our cross, (surrendering our way for His way) or to get on our knees in prayer. The truth is, we are not so thrilled about suffering. We don't want pain. We don't want to feel bad. We don't want discomfort. We want to feel good, and we want to feel good now. We certainly also don't want to be told what we can and can't do. After all, it's in our nature to think of ourselves above all things.

The Christian Lifestyle comes at a cost. The cross, although we see it as a symbol of pain and suffering, it is really about death. Death to our own plans. Even Jesus, pleading to not die on the cross in His humanity, gave up what he wanted for what the father wanted. This is what he meant when he said, "Not my will, but yours be done." We can't keep doing what we've always done, feeling empty and expecting different results. To experience life, we have to stay connected to our life source. This message is for those who have made that commitment to Christ. If you are reading this and have not done that, you will have an opportunity at the end of this chapter. If God is prompting you now, by all means, jump to the end and then come back to this spot.

Christian and non-Christian alike are under the chains of the feel good addiction as long as we are but flesh and blood. The difference for the Christian feel good addict is that Christians have access to a supercharged supernatural power called the Holy Spirit. When Jesus ascended to heaven after his resurrection from the dead (what Easter is really about), he gathered his followers together and he "breathed on them and said, receive the Holy Spirit."(John 20:22). It is an infilling of the spirit of God that gives us the ability to forgive, make changes and face difficulty with peace. It also allows us to rise out of difficulty with a supernatural strength that often cannot be explained. Many Christians, however, fail to tap into it. Instead we flounder, struggle, and give in no differently than those who have not accepted and received Christ. If we handle life the same as though who do not know Christ, why would they want to? What is the difference?

In David Timms' book *Sacred Waiting*, he writes "in the midst of our mad scramble—what we bravely but vainly call the "good life"—we also find ourselves harboring deep-seated impatience with God. We have little time to nurture a relationship with Him and generally feel that He should run at least as fast as we do. If we have a problem right now, then right now would be a good time for the Lord to step in and deal with it."

God does indeed want to help us. The problem is we think we know in which way and when He should do so. We looked briefly at how the feel good addict can have a negative effect on relationships. Our relationship with Jesus needs the same intentional attention for it to be sound. How it must break His heart when we cry out to God to help us, then tell Him to stay away when we want to do what we want to do, when we want to do it.

In the Book of Revelation, Chapter 3, there is a letter to the church in Laodicea. It says how God wishes that they were either hot or cold, but since they were just lukewarm, God will spit them out of his mouth. Ouch! I can guess that in today's terms, the lukewarm Christian is another name for the settling for good enough, the status quo and the comfort zone of complacent Christianity. We want our cake (salvation) and the freedom to eat it when we want to (following Christ).

Confession: *There was a period of about four years where I rarely read my Bible. In fact, I just couldn't seem to get regular at all. I would occasionally read a devotional or some anecdotes, but that was about it. I also wasn't journaling, although was once an avid journaler of thoughts and prayers. Those years were flat. It seemed that God was far away and silent. I had very little ambition to dig deep. I was tired, beaten down and worn out. I had spent so many years prior to that time diving in and going* *deep with God, staying connected until I got wounded by my church. This blow sucked all the wind out of my sails. As a result, I spent more time in front of the television, less on reading, praying and much less on being active. I honestly didn't care most of the time. Some days I would weep and then get a burst of energy and then would get knocked down when the smallest of negativity turned my way. I became ambivalent and depressed. I gained weight, and then it became a game of trying to destroy myself. I wondered just how fat I could get. This was totally out of character. Being a couch potato wasn't something I thought was in my DNA. I had pursued God relentlessly through a great deal of personal trauma and difficulty. But here I was. I had given up. I just wanted to have a life that was full of ease, no striving, no should do's, have to's, or must do's. Eventually the hole I was in was so deep, when I wanted out, I couldn't find my way. The life I thought I wanted wasn't it at all. I wanted 'me' back. The ambitious, relentless, tenacious, positive, I-can-do-anything-with-God person. I realized that I had become lukewarm. I felt like God was spitting me out. He seemed far away. The truth was, it was I who was far away.*

That day I made a choice. To pray, read my Bible, and pursue God with all that was in me, even when I didn't feel like it. It didn't take long to feel close to God again. But it did take about four years to feel somewhat back to normal. I don't take that relationship for granted anymore. It's like quitting caffeine or sugar. When you stop, you deal with a headache and cravings. Then before you know it, all that is gone and you feel like a million bucks and never want to face those withdrawals again. Like the story of the man getting the transfusion, when we are distant from God, we feel weak and sick. If that is you today, stop reading and tell Him you're sorry and reconnect with Him.

The feel good addict in us is cunning and sly. It distracts us from being consistent. In our lack of prayer, listening, seeking, Bible reading, trusting, attending church, or any kind of isolation from anything resembling organized religion. Why? Because it takes time, effort and intention. It might take forgiveness from being wounded by a church. Trust me when I say I get that one all too well. Those are not easy things to overcome. But they can be overcome. It takes being honest with God, asking for strength and quite possibly the 'D' word…discipline and definitely consistency, all of which are aversions of the feel good addict.

The consequences of being a feel good addict in the Christian life is equal to that of those who are not Christians. God is not partial. The feel good Christian may wonder why they feel joyless. God might feel far away and distant. It might feel as if prayers fall on deaf ears, bringing on feelings of being purposeless and abandoned. Difficulties might seem to keep coming, and people might feel as if they are being buried with no reprieve in sight. The feel good addict Christian might wonder why they keep facing the same difficulties over and over. They might even begin to be cynical, asking themselves why should they continue with God and Christianity when it seems like it doesn't do anything for them but create problems.

Years ago a woman said to me that if God didn't want her to eat chocolate, then He needed to take away the desire. That made as much sense as saying if God didn't want me to fly, he would stop me from jumping off a cliff. If we removed God from the equation just for a moment, we will see that this logic makes no sense. If God was not available to blame for our difficulties, addictions or other negative things that occur in our lives, who would be responsible?

God is not a genie. He is not a dictator, nor is he an authoritarian leaving us with no explanations for what He asks us to do and be with Him. He has given us an amazing gift called free will. It is available to all, Christian or not. But the Christian, the one who made a public proclamation to accept Christ as their Savior, to receive the gift of eternal life, is asked to continually make a choice every day after that moment and for the rest of their lives on this earth. The feel good addict has to be put to death (on our own mini cross) every minute of every day. The good news is, as a Christian, you don't have to work at it alone. This is where the Holy Spirit does its best work. Jesus said in John 14 that "the Advocate, the Holy Spirit, whom the Father will send in my name, will teach you all things and will remind you of everything I have said to you." In Ephesians three, the Apostle Paul prays this prayer for all: "I pray that out of his glorious riches he may strengthen you with power through his Spirit in your inner being, so that Christ may dwell in your hearts through faith."

This is where the Christian has an advantage to overcome the feel good addict, yet so often fails to tap into this power. Instead, they adopt the same attitude as those who don't know Christ. The mindset of instant gratification is the most conflicting with the Christian lifestyle. We want what we want and we want it now. We want great relationship with God that doesn't infringe or cramp our lifestyle, one that doesn't ask me to do things that are uncomfortable, one that doesn't conflict with my own adopted principles and values or challenge my desires. That's the human nature way of the feel good addict. But the Christian life is set apart differently and not to be the same as the world around us. We are in it, but not to be of it.

The way we fool ourselves is no different than anyone else but with a spiritual flavor to it. We might say things like, "I am under grace, God understands my busy schedule," or "I don't need to pray, God already knows what I need," and my favorite, "God loves me just the way I am." All of those statements are true. The catch is they all say to God that we have decided what it means to be a Christian and in relationship with God, instead of what God tells us. In a way, it is kind of a repeat of the Garden of Eden.

Grace is no license to do as we please, when we please, and for as long as we please. As God's creation, we are made to serve our Creator. In the absence of truth, we will serve somebody or something. Our only choice in this matter is who will we serve? Our feel good addict or God? The only way we know what to do is to stay in constant contact with the Creator. In first Thessalonians chapter five, these simple words are said to us: "Pray continually". The reason is captured perfectly in second Timothy chapter four, "For the time will come when people will not put up with sound teaching. Instead, to suit their own desires, they will gather around them a great number of teachers to say what their itching ears want to hear." Therefore my fellow Christian and struggling feel good addict, "Be on your guard; stand firm in the faith; be courageous; be strong."[25]

God indeed does love us as we are, but that is only the beginning. He knows that as we are, is less than what we can be. Our relationship with Him is crucial in discovering our

---

[25] 1 Corinthians 16:13 NIV

purpose and calling and learning how to best navigate life. Without Him, we will flounder and flop. He wants relationship with us so badly, that it killed Him. How sad to continue to kill him day after day by avoiding Him. It is impossible to have a relationship with someone as we saw, while thinking only of ourselves. Eventually the other party will feel you are not really interested in a relationship, and after repeated attempts to connect with you, they might just let you go off and do your own thing. The book of Romans, chapter one verse twenty eight gravely and sadly captures the outcome for us in this situation. "Since they thought it foolish to acknowledge God, he abandoned them to their foolish thinking and let them do things that should never be done."[26] That would be a sad day for your God who loves you.

The preceding paragraphs may have sounded pretty rough, but remember, this is a book about being honest. I have been in this space and it was pretty miserable. It is amazing to me how easily we fool ourselves when, if we just stop for one minute in our self-deception, we will realize how silly we sound. If you want a great life, get real with yourself. Right now is a good time to have a little spiritual honesty.

Some questions for reflection:

1. How frequently and how much do you read your Bible?

2. What is your prayer life like?

3. What do you get out of attending church? If you do not attend a church, what is your reasoning?

4. What made you accept Christ?

---

[26] Romans 1:28 NLT

5. What does "take up your cross and follow Jesus" mean to you?

6. What does it mean to you to be a Christian?

When you have finished your self-evaluation, read on for practical ways to get the upper hand on your feel good addict.

Confession: *I was taking a break before I got back to writing one day. I had made some lunch, sat down, and turned on the television while I ate. There was a rerun of the show Blue Bloods on. When I finished eating, I sat for a few minutes. When I got up to put my dishes in the sink, I actually had a thought that it would be rude of me and disrespectful to the Reagan family (the fictional television family that I had gotten so familiar with) to turn off the show before it ended. I'm not kidding! I turned it off anyway, but wondered why that thought popped in my head.*

I believe that thought was there because I got so wrapped up in the programs characters' lives that they became real to me, and a source of fellowship. After a brief evaluation and reflection, I realized the powerful yet subtle influence television was having on my reality of what true relationship was about. Those relationships end after the series ends. God never ends.

Practical tools for the Christian feel good addict

If you have allowed your feel good addict to have more control in your life and God has taken a backseat, to get that flipped around you need to start small to assure your success. It's easy to set ourselves up for failure with the all-or-nothing mindset. I recommend starting with good, then move to better, and finally to best.

Let's begin with good. For the first week, start with practicing talking to God like you would a friend. Don't use Christian-ese words like sanctify, justify, and edify and flower it all up. God doesn't much care for a flowery vocabulary. Just say, "Hey God, it's me" and let it go from there. God speaks our language. He reminds us how to pray in Matthew chapter six, verses five and six: "And when you pray, do not be like the hypocrites. For they love to pray standing in the synagogues and on the street corners to be seen by men. Truly I tell you, they already have their reward. But when you pray, go into your inner room, shut your door, and pray to your Father, who is unseen, and your Father, who sees what is done in secret, will reward you."[27]

For the second week, add on taking a few minutes after chatting with Him to just listen. Close your eyes to block out distractions. Quiet your thoughts and just say 'speak to me, I'm listening.' Then wait. For most people, this is probably the hardest of all. We start thinking, making lists in our head and planning out our next activity. Stretch yourself. Try it for two minutes at first. You can do it.

For week three, add on reading one chapter in the New Testament a day. If you are a devotional reader, stop reading those for this three week period. That is someone else's experiences with God. Live *your* life with Him. By week three, you will spend about fifteen to thirty minutes a day combining all these actions. Everyone has the same sixteen hours a day to spend awake. Set yourself up for a good success and block out thirty minutes so you don't start stressing about the time.

---

[27] Matthew 6:5-6 NIV

When you are ready to move onto better, or already are at this place, you don't necessarily have to add on more time. You can still have a significant experience with God in thirty dedicated minutes. Let's kick up the reading though. Keep reading one chapter in the New Testament, then add ten verses in Psalms, two verses in Proverbs and two paragraphs in the Old Testament. That will take you about ten to fifteen minutes. (For a bit of help and a structured reading plan, see the end of the book).

Before you read, ask God to open up what you read to your mind and heart. Then read your passages for the day followed by a conversation with God. Talk about your thoughts on what you read, and then listen for His response — just like having a conversation. If you haven't already, start attending a church once a week even it if is online. Preferably a Bible-teaching church that is growing. Sometimes you might have to hop a bit to find the right fit for you. Better yet, ask God to show you where to attend.

Be intentional in your relationship. Don't be afraid to talk to Him or ask Him for even the simplest things. Check in with Him, making an effort to stay in constant contact in conversation. Speak your prayers out loud, even if it is a whisper. There is something powerful about getting it out of our head and through our mouths.

For the most relational experience with God, don't be afraid to have those hard conversations with Him. The things you struggle with. The things that make you mad, sad, happy and joyful. The most effective way to keep our feel good addict in check is to have constant contact with the one who is bigger, better and stronger than us – God. If you want to eat or do something that has been hard for you to say no to, ask God and the Holy Spirit for help. Get specific. Yes, He knows anyway, but He wants to make sure you know. When we acknowledge it out loud the thing that feels so huge and hard to overcome, becomes less powerful and loses its hold over us.

By this time you should have a pretty good ear tuned to His voice. Take the amazing foundation that is built and let God continue to build on it. Get connected with your church or other organizations that offers a weekly Bible study in addition to your weekend or online service. Use the Bible reading plan at the end of this chapter or get any of the many apps available for smartphones, or search the Internet for a Bible reading plan. I find that is the best way to stay consistent. I use the one year Bible reading plan found on a Bible app that is the same as the one I have included in this book. I have used this method for years, and if you find yourself in a pinch to sit and read, you can use the audible portion of the app and listen to the readings for that day. Another way to get connected is through journaling, or at least writing down specific prayers.

One powerful way to capture your prayers and see the powerful hand of God at work is to find a wall or closet wall to hang your prayers on and periodically reflect on them. It will amaze you to see how God answers you. It is things like this that build your faith, your depth, and develops your intimacy with God.

If you would like to receive the life giving transfusion of Christ, simply pray this prayer:

"God, I recognize that I have not lived my life for You up until now. I have been living for myself. I need You in my life; I want You in my life. I acknowledge what Your Son Jesus Christ did in giving His life for me on the cross and I want to receive the forgiveness you offer and the new start that comes from knowing you. I ask you to come into my life now, Lord. From this day forward, I will do all that is in my power to stay close to you and trust you that when I am weak in doing that, you will help me stay on my feet, or will come and carry me. Thank you for loving me and caring enough for what is best for my life. Help me to follow you, to trust you and to honor you. In Jesus Name. Amen.

Conclusion

I don't know what prompted you to pick up this book. Maybe you have felt stuck and couldn't find your way out. Maybe you have been in limbo and needed a push. Or perhaps you felt you had it all together and were just curious about the title. Whatever got you here, I hope it has been as an enlightening journey as it has been for me writing it.

I will be honest, this was a challenging book to write. It brought out areas in which I had no idea I even had a feel good addict. These areas, in spite of some good efforts, were very much alive and well. This book has inspired and motivated me to take my own advice and make some changes.

I don't know what your feel good addict entails. This book only covered a few areas. When I was younger, someone asked me if I was in the military because I was so disciplined. But really, I wasn't. I was obsessed with not disappointing others. That was just a different type of feel good addict. One that sought perfection and approval. The feel good addict comes in all shapes and sizes. It's the selfish side of all of us that may crave sheer comfort or total emotional protection.

The beauty I found in writing this book has been encapsulated in the quote I mentioned earlier by Carl Jung: "Until you make the unconscious conscious, it will direct your life and you will call it fate." In the first chapter I challenged you to take a snapshot of your life as it was at that moment.

If you have that available, I encourage you to take it out and read it and answer these questions:

1. In what ways did your thinking shift?

2. What changes did you or are you making to reduce the affect your feel good addict has on others?

3. What changes in your life did you or are you making for the positive?

It is my hope that you experienced a shift for the positive, that you became aware where you may have been unconscious and saw ways where you could make a difference in your little corner of the world. If you have been stuck in a dead-end job, I pray that you found your wings to fly. Whatever your feel good addict is or has been, it is my hope that it was identified, exposed and you took back control over your life. I hope the truths found in this book literally set you free from the bondage of the status quo, the good enough, and the trappings of the comfort zone.

It is never fun or pleasurable to shine a light on the areas in our lives that we conceal, especially those we conceal from ourselves. As I wrote this book, I found it was easy to think of others having issues while parts of myself were hidden. But that which stays hidden only serves to keep us trapped and in bondage. It is only when the light of truth illuminates us that we will be able to truly find the path that will set us free.

It's time to step out and live my friends. Life inside the comfort zone is no place to exist. It is empty, dark and lonely. Settling for good enough is not good enough for you. Find out why you are here. What you want in life? Don't let your feel good addict keep you living a life that is less than what you were created for.

Go out and be a friend, be a good worker, be a helpful neighbor. Love your pets. Don't let your feel good addict have control in your life. Start with good, then move to better and finally to best.

Thank you for taking this journey with me.

How I did it!

Have you ever wanted to be an author? I did to. For years! I felt overwhelmed with what to do, how to start, how to market and everything else *how to*! That is when I found the Self-Publishing School. So, if you are like me and are reading this and thinking, *"I want to write a book"*, then read on! Self-Publishing School helped me, and now I want them to help you.

Even if you're too busy, bad at writing or like me, don't know where to start, you *CAN* write a bestseller and build your best life.

With tools and experience across a variety of niches and professions, Self-Publishing School is the only resource you will need to take your book (or the one that is in you waiting to be written) to the finish line and you becoming a published author.

Don't keep wondering if you can do it…

YOU CAN!

To help get you started, watch the FREE video series now, by clicking below. I did it and I keep pinching myself that you are reading my book…the one I never thought I would write, finish, or much less publish. Today is your day to say *YES* to you and yes to *YOU* becoming a bestselling author. I look forward to reading your book!

Click (or copy this link) to get started!

https://xe172.isrefer.com/go/curcust/bookbrosinc3015

One Year Bible Reading Plan

These readings take only fifteen minutes a day! This unique plan was arranged by the Tyndale House Publishers – and you can purchase their "One Year Bible" or use their plan (shown below) with your own Bible. Each of the 365 daily readings includes a portion from the Old Testament, the New Testament, Psalms, and Proverbs. It is an exciting approach to taking in the whole bible . . . each year!

__ Jan. 1 Genesis 1:1 – 2:25 Matthew 1:1 – 2:12 Ps. 1:1-6 Prov. 1:1-6

__ Jan. 2 Genesis 3:1 – 4:26 Matthew 2:13 – 3:6 Ps. 2:1-12 Prov. 1:7-9

__ Jan. 3 Genesis 5:1 – 7:24 Matthew 3:7 – 4:11 Ps. 3:1-8 Prov. 1:10-19

__ Jan. 4 Genesis 8:1 – 10:32 Matthew 4:12 – 25 Ps. 4:1-8 Prov. 1:20-23

__ Jan. 5 Genesis 11:1 – 13:4 Matthew 5:1-26 Ps. 5:1-12 Prov. 1:24-28

__ Jan. 6 Genesis 13:5 – 15:21 Matthew 5:27-48 Ps. 6:1-10 Prov. 1:29-33

__ Jan. 7 Genesis 16:1 – 18:19 Matthew 6:1 – 24 Ps. 7:1-17 Prov. 2:1-5

__ Jan. 8 Genesis 18:20 – 19:38 Matthew 6:25 – 7:14 Ps. 8:1-9 Prov. 2:6-15

__ Jan. 9 Genesis 20:1 – 22:24 Matthew 7:15 – 29 Ps. 9:1-12 Prov. 2:16-22

__ Jan. 10 Genesis 23:1 – 24:51 Matthew 8:1 – 17 Ps. 9: 13-20 Prov. 3:1-6

__ Jan. 11 Genesis 24:52 – 26:16 Matthew 8:18-34 Ps. 10:1-15 Prov. 3:7-8

__ Jan. 12 Genesis 26:17 – 27:46 Matthew 9:1 – 17 Ps. 10:16-18 Prov. 3:9-10

__ Jan. 13 Genesis 28:1 – 29:35 Matthew 9:18 – 38 Ps. 11:1-7 Prov. 3:11-12

__ Jan. 14 Genesis 30:1 – 31:16 Matthew 10:1 – 25 Ps. 12:1-8 Prov. 3:13-15

__ Jan. 15 Genesis 31:17 – 32:12 Matthew 10:26 – 11:6 Ps. 13:1-6 Prov. 3:16-18

__ Jan. 16 Genesis 32:13 – 34:31 Matthew 11:7 – 30 Ps. 14:1-7 Prov. 3:19-20

__ Jan. 17 Genesis 35:1 – 36:43 Matthew 12:1 – 21 Ps. 15:1-5 Prov. 3:21-26

__ Jan. 18 Genesis 37:1 – 38:30 Matthew 12:22 – 45 Ps. 16:1-11 Prov. 3:27-32

__ Jan. 19 Genesis 39:1 – 41:16 Matthew 12:46 – 13:23 Ps. 17:1-15 Prov. 3:33-35

__ Jan. 20 Genesis 41:17 – 42:17 Matthew 13:24 – 46 Ps. 18:1-15 Prov. 4:1-6

__ Jan. 21 Genesis 42:18 – 43:34 Matthew 13:47 – 14:12 Ps. 18:16-36 Prov. 4:7-10

__ Jan. 22 Genesis 44:1 – 45:28 Matthew 14:13 – 36 Ps. 18: 37-50 Prov. 4:11-13

__ Jan. 23 Genesis 46:1 – 47: 31 Matthew 15:1 – 28 Ps. 19:1-14 Prov. 4:14-19

__ Jan. 24 Genesis 48:1 – 49:33 Matthew 15:29 – 16:12 Ps. 20:1-9 Prov. 4:20-27

__ Jan. 25 Gen. 50:1 – Ex. 2:10 Matthew 16:13 – 17:9 Ps. 21:1-13 Prov. 5:1-6

__ Jan. 26 Exodus 2:11 – 3:22 Matthew 17:10 – 27 Ps. 22:1-18 Prov. 5:7-14
__ Jan. 27 Exodus 4:1 – 5:21 Matthew 18:1 – 22 Ps. 22:19-31 Prov. 5:15-21
__ Jan. 28 Exodus 5:22 – 7:24 Matthew 18:23 – 19:12 Ps. 23:1-6 Prov. 5:22-23
__ Jan. 29 Exodus 7:25 – 9:35 Matthew 19:13 – 30 Ps. 24:1-10 Prov. 6:1-5
__ Jan. 30 Exodus 10:1 – 12:13 Matthew 20:1 – 28 Ps. 25:1 – 15 Prov. 6:6-11
__ Jan. 31 Exodus 12:14 – 13:16 Matthew 20:29 – 21:22 Ps. 25:16-22 Prov. 6:12-15

__ Feb. 1 Exodus 13:17 – 15:18 Matthew 21:23 – 46 Ps. 26:1-12 Prov. 6:16-19
__ Feb. 2 Exodus 15:19 – 17:7 Matthew 22:1 – 33 Ps. 27:1-6 Prov. 6:20-26
__ Feb. 3 Exodus 17:8 – 19:15 Matthew 22:34 – 23:12 Ps. 27:7-14 Prov. 6:27-35
__ Feb. 4 Exodus 19:16 – 21:21 Matthew 23:13 –39 Ps. 28:1-9 Prov. 7:1-5
__ Feb. 5 Exodus 21:22 – 23:13 Matthew 24:1 - 28 Ps. 29:1-11 Prov. 7:6-23
__ Feb. 6 Exodus 23:14 – 25:40 Matthew 24:29 – 51 Ps. 30:1-12 Prov. 7:24-27
__ Feb. 7 Exodus 26:1 – 27:21 Matthew 25:1 – 30 Ps. 31:1-8 Prov. 8:1-11
__ Feb. 8 Exodus 28:1 – 43 Matthew 25:31 – 26:13 Ps. 31:9-18 Prov. 8:12-13
__ Feb. 9 Exodus 29:1 – 30:10 Matthew 26:14 –46 Ps. 31:19 –24 Prov. 8:14-26
__ Feb. 10 Exodus 30:11 – 31:18 Matthew 26:47 – 68 Ps. 32:1-11 Prov. 8:27-32
__ Feb. 11 Exodus 32:1 – 33:23 Matthew 26:69 – 27:14 Ps. 33:1-11 Prov. 8:33-36
__ Feb. 12 Exodus 34:1 – 35:9 Matthew 27:15 – 31 Ps. 33:12-22 Prov. 9:1-6
__ Feb. 13 Exodus 35:10 – 36:38 Matthew 27:32 – 66 Ps. 34:1-10 Prov. 9:7-8
__ Feb. 14 Exodus 37:1 – 38:31 Matthew 28:1 – 20 Ps. 34:11-22 Prov. 9:9-10
__ Feb. 15 Exodus 39:1 – 40:38 Mark 1:1 – 28 Ps. 35:1-16 Prov. 9:11-12
__ Feb. 16 Leviticus 1:1 – 3:17 Mark 1:29 – 2:12 Ps. 35:17-28 Prov. 9:13-18
__ Feb. 17 Leviticus 4:1 – 5:19 Mark 2:13 – 3:6 Ps. 36:1-12 Prov. 10:1-2
__ Feb. 18 Leviticus 6:1 – 7:27 Mark 3:7 – 30 Ps. 37:1-11 Prov. 10:3-4
__ Feb. 19 Leviticus 7:28 – 9:6 Mark 3:31 – 4:25 Ps. 37:12-29 Prov. 10:5
__ Feb. 20 Leviticus 9:7 – 10:20 Mark 4:26 – 5:20 Ps. 37:30-40 Prov. 10:6-7
__ Feb. 21 Leviticus 11:1 – 12:8 Mark 5:21 – 43 Ps. 38:1-22 Prov. 10:8-9
__ Feb. 22 Leviticus 13:1 – 59 Mark 6:1 – 29 Ps. 39:1-13 Prov. 10:10
__ Feb. 23 Leviticus 14:1 – 57 Mark 6:30 – 56 Ps. 40:1-10 Prov. 10:11-12
__ Feb. 24 Leviticus 15:1 – 16:28 Mark 7:1-23 Ps. 40:11-17 Prov. 10:13-14
__ Feb. 25 Leviticus 16:29 – 18:30 Mark 7:24 – 8:10 Ps. 41:1-13 Prov. 10:15-16
__ Feb. 26 Leviticus 19:1 – 20:21 Mark 8:11 – 38 Ps. 42:1-11 Prov. 10:17
__ Feb. 27 Leviticus 20:22 – 22:16 Mark 9:1 –29 Ps. 43:1-5 Prov. 10:18
__ Feb. 28 Leviticus 22:17 – 23:44 Mark 9:30 – 10:12 Ps. 44:1-8 Prov. 10:19

__ Mar. 1 Leviticus 24:1 – 25:46 Mark 10:13 – 31 Ps. 44:9-26 Prov. 10:20-21
__ Mar. 2 Leviticus 25:47 – 27:13 Mark 10:32 – 52 Ps. 45:1-17 Prov. 10:22
__ Mar. 3 Lev. 27:14 – Num. 1:54 Mark 11:1 – 26 Ps. 46:1-11 Prov. 10:23
__ Mar. 4 Numbers 2:1 – 3:51 Mark 11:27 – 12:17 Ps. 47:1-9 Prov. 10:24-25

__ Mar. 5 Numbers 4:1 – 5:31 Mark 12:18 – 37 Ps. 48:1-14 Prov. 10:26
__ Mar. 6 Numbers 6:1 – 7:89 Mark 12:38 – 13:13 Ps. 49:1-20 Prov. 10:27-28
__ Mar. 7 Numbers 8:1 – 9:23 Mark 13:14 – 37 Ps. 50:1-23 Prov. 10:29-30
__ Mar. 8 Numbers 10:1 – 11:23 Mark 14:1 – 21 Ps. 51:1-19 Prov. 10:31-32
__ Mar. 9 Numbers 11:24 – 13:33 Mark 14:22 – 52 Ps. 52:1-9 Prov. 11:1-3
__ Mar. 10 Numbers 14:1 – 15:16 Mark 14:53 – 72 Ps. 53:1-6 Prov. 11:4
__ Mar. 11 Numbers 15:17 – 16:40 Mark 15:1 – 47 Ps. 54:1-7 Prov. 11:5-6
__ Mar. 12 Numbers 16:41 – 18:32 Mark 16:1 – 20 Ps. 55:1-23 Prov. 11:7
__ Mar. 13 Numbers 19:1 – 20:29 Luke 1:1 – 25 Ps. 56:1-13 Prov. 11:8
__ Mar. 14 Numbers 21:1 – 22:20 Luke 1:26 – 56 Ps. 57:1-11 Prov. 11:9-11
__ Mar. 15 Numbers 22:21 – 23:30 Luke 1:57 – 80 Ps. 58:1 –11 Prov. 11:12-13
__ Mar. 16 Numbers 24:1 – 25:18 Luke 2:1 – 35 Ps. 59:1-17 Prov. 11:14
__ Mar. 17 Numbers 26:1 – 51 Luke 2:36 – 52 Ps. 60:1-12 Prov. 11:15
__ Mar. 18 Numbers 26:52 – 28:15 Luke 3:1 – 22 Ps. 61:1-8 Prov. 11:16-17
__ Mar. 19 Numbers 28:16 – 29:40 Luke 3:23 –38 Ps. 62:1 –12 Prov. 11:18-19
__ Mar. 20 Numbers 30:1 – 31:54 Luke 4:1 – 30 Ps. 63:1-11 Prov. 11:20-21
__ Mar. 21 Numbers 32:1 – 33:39 Luke 4:31 – 5:11 Ps. 64:1 –10 Prov. 11:22
__ Mar. 22 Numbers 33:40 – 35:34 Luke 5:12 – 28 Ps. 65:1-13 Prov. 11:23
__ Mar. 23 Num. 36:1 – Deut. 1:46 Luke 5:29 – 6:11 Ps. 66:1-20 Prov. 11:24-26
__ Mar. 24 Deuteronomy 2:1 – 3:29 Luke 6:12 – 38 Ps. 67:1-7 Prov. 11:27
__ Mar. 25 Deuteronomy 4:1–49 Luke 6:39 – 7:10 Ps. 68:1-18 Prov. 11:28
__ Mar. 26 Deuteronomy 5:1 – 6:25 Luke 7:11 – 35 Ps. 68:19-35 Prov. 11:29-31
__ Mar. 27 Deuteronomy 7:1 – 8:20 Luke 7:36 – 8:3 Ps. 69:1-18 Prov. 12:1
__ Mar. 28 Deuteronomy 9:1 – 10:22 Luke 8:4 – 21 Ps. 69:19-36 Prov. 12:2-3
__ Mar. 29 Deuteronomy 11:1 –12:32 Luke 8:22 – 39 Ps. 70:1-5 Prov. 12:4
__ Mar. 30 Deuteronomy 13:1 –15:23 Luke 8:40 – 9:6 Ps. 71:1-24 Prov. 12:5-7
__ Mar. 31 Deuteronomy 16:1 – 17:20 Luke 9:7 – 27 Ps. 72:1-20 Prov. 12:8-9

__ Apr. 1 Deuteronomy 18:1 – 20:20 Luke 9:28 – 50 Ps. 73:1-28 Prov. 12:10
__ Apr. 2 Deuteronomy 21:1 – 22:30 Luke 9:51 – 10:12 Ps. 74:1-23 Prov. 12:11
__ Apr. 3 Deuteronomy 23:1 – 25:19 Luke 10:13 – 37 Ps. 75:1-10 Prov. 12:12-14
__ Apr. 4 Deuteronomy 26:1 – 27:26 Luke 10:38 –11:13 Ps. 76:1-12 Prov.12:15-17
__ Apr. 5 Deuteronomy 28:1–68 Luke 11:14 – 36 Ps. 77:1-20 Prov. 12:18
__ Apr. 6 Deuteronomy 29:1 – 30:20 Luke 11:37 – 12:7 Ps. 78:1-31 Prov. 12:19-20
__ Apr. 7 Deuteronomy 31:1 – 32:27 Luke 12:8 – 34 Ps. 78:32-55 Prov. 12:21-23
__ Apr. 8 Deuteronomy 32:28 – 52 Luke 12:35 – 59 Ps. 78:56-64 Prov. 12:24
__ Apr. 9 Deuteronomy 33:1–29 Luke 13:1 – 21 Ps. 78:65-72 Prov. 12:25
__ Apr. 10 Deut. 34:1 – Joshua 2:24 Luke 13:22 – 14:6 Ps. 79:1-13 Prov. 12:26
__ Apr. 11 Joshua 3:1 – 4:24 Luke 14:7 – 35 Ps. 80:1-19 Prov. 12:27-28
__ Apr. 12 Joshua 5:1 – 7:15 Luke 15:1 – 32 Ps. 81:1-16 Prov. 13:1
__ Apr. 13 Joshua 7:16 – 9:2 Luke 16:1 – 18 Ps. 82:1-8 Prov. 13:2-3

__ Apr. 14 Joshua 9:3 – 10:43 Luke 16:19 – 17:10 Ps. 83:1-18 Prov. 13:4

__ Apr. 15 Joshua 11:1 – 12:24 Luke 17:11 – 37 Ps. 84:1-12 Prov. 13:5-6

__ Apr. 16 Joshua 13:1 – 14:15 Luke 18:1 – 17 Ps. 85:1-13 Prov. 13:7-8

__ Apr. 17 Joshua 15:1 – 63 Luke 18:18 – 43 Ps. 86:1-17 Prov. 13:9-10

__ Apr. 18 Joshua 16:1 – 18:28 Luke 19:1 – 27 Ps. 87:1-7 Prov. 13:11

__ Apr. 19 Joshua 19:1 – 20:9 Luke 19:28 – 48 Ps. 88:1-18 Prov. 13:12-14

__ Apr. 20 Joshua 21:1 – 22:20 Luke 20:1 – 26 Ps. 89:1-13 Prov. 13:15-16

__ Apr. 21 Joshua 22:21 – 23:16 Luke 20:27 – 47 Ps. 89:14-37 Prov. 13:17-19

__ Apr. 22 Joshua 24:1 – 33 Luke 21:1 – 28 Ps. 89:38-52 Prov. 13:20-23

__ Apr. 23 Judges 1:1 – 2:9 Luke 21:29 – 22:13 Ps. 90:1 – 91:16 Prov. 13:24-25

__ Apr. 24 Judges 2:10 – 3:31 Luke 22:14 –34 Ps. 92:1 – 93:5 Prov. 14:1-2

__ Apr. 25 Judges 4:1 – 5:31 Luke 22:35 – 53 Ps. 94:1-23 Prov. 14:3-4

__ Apr. 26 Judges 6:1 – 40 Luke 22:54 – 23:12 Ps. 95:1 – 96:13 Prov. 14:5-6

__ Apr. 27 Judges 7:1 – 8:17 Luke 23:13 – 43 Ps. 97:1 – 98:9 Prov. 14:7-8

__ Apr. 28 Judges 8:18 – 9:21 Luke 23:44 – 24:12 Ps. 99:1-9 Prov. 14:9-10

__ Apr. 29 Judges 9:22 – 10:18 Luke 24:13 – 53 Ps. 100:1-5 Prov. 14:11-12

__ Apr. 30 Judges 11:1 – 12:15 John 1:1 – 28 Ps. 101:1-8 Prov. 14:13-14

__ May 1 Judges 13:1 – 14:20 John 1:29 – 51 Ps. 102:1-28 Prov. 14:15-16

__ May 2 Judges 15:1 – 16:31 John 2:1 – 25 Ps. 103:1-22 Prov. 14:17-19

__ May 3 Judges 17:1 – 18:31 John 3:1 – 21 Ps. 104:1-23 Prov. 14:20-21

__ May 4 Judges 19:1 – 20:48 John 3:22 – 4:3 Ps. 104:24-35 Prov. 14:22-24

__ May 5 Judges 21:1 – Ruth 1:22 John 4:4 – 42 Ps. 105:1-15 Prov. 14:25

__ May 6 Ruth 2:1 – 4:22 John 4:43 – 54 Ps. 105:16-36 Prov. 14:26-27

__ May 7 1 Samuel 1:1 – 2:21 John 5:1 – 23 Ps. 105:37-45 Prov. 14:28-29

__ May 8 1 Samuel 2:22 – 4:22 John 5:24 – 47 Ps. 106:1-12 Prov. 14:30-31

__ May 9 1 Samuel 5:1 – 7:17 John 6:1 – 21 Ps. 106:13-31 Prov. 14:32-33

__ May 10 1 Samuel 8:1 – 9:27 John 6:22 – 42 Ps. 106:32-48 Prov. 14:34-35

__ May 11 1 Samuel 10:1 – 11:15 John 6:43 – 71 Ps. 107:1-43 Prov. 15:1-3

__ May 12 1 Samuel 12:1 – 13:22 John 7:1 – 29 Ps. 108:1-13 Prov. 15:4

__ May 13 1 Samuel 13:23 – 14:52 John 7:30 – 53 Ps. 109:1-31 Prov. 15:5-7

__ May 14 1 Samuel 15:1 – 16:23 John 8:1 – 20 Ps. 110:1-7 Prov. 15:8-10

__ May 15 1 Samuel 17:1 – 18:4 John 8:21 – 30 Ps. 111:1-10 Prov. 15:11

__ May 16 1 Samuel 18:5 – 19:24 John 8:31 – 59 Ps. 112:1-10 Prov. 15:12-14

__ May 17 1 Samuel 20:1 – 21:15 John 9:1 – 41 Ps. 113:1-114:8 Prov. 15:15-17

__ May 18 1 Samuel 22:1 – 23:29 John 10:1 – 21 Ps. 115:1-18 Prov. 15:18-19

__ May 19 1 Samuel 24:1 – 25:44 John 10:22 – 42 Ps. 116:1-19 Prov. 15:20-21

__ May 20 1 Samuel 26:1 – 28:25 John 11:1 – 53 Ps. 117:1-2 Prov. 15:22-23

__ May 21 1 Samuel 29:1 – 31:13 John 11:54 – 12:19 Ps. 118:1-18 Prov. 15:24-26

__ May 22 2 Samuel 1:1 – 2:11 John 12:20 – 50 Ps. 118:19-29 Prov. 15:27-28

__ May 23 2 Samuel 2:12 – 3:39 John 13:1 – 30 Ps. 119:1-16 Prov. 15:29-30

__ May 24 2 Samuel 4:1 – 6:23 John 13:31 – 14:14 Ps. 119:17-32 Prov. 15:31-32
__ May 25 2 Samuel 7:1 – 8:18 John 14:15 – 31 Ps. 119:33-48 Prov. 15:33
__ May 26 2 Samuel 9:1 – 11:27 John 15:1 – 27 Ps. 119:49-64 Prov. 16:1-3
__ May 27 2 Samuel 12:1 – 31 John 16:1 – 33 Ps. 119:65-80 Prov. 16:4-5
__ May 28 2 Samuel 13:1 - 39 John 17:1 - 26 Ps. 119:81-96 Prov. 16:6-7
__ May 29 2 Samuel 14:1 – 15:22 John 18:1 – 24 Ps. 119:97-112 Prov. 16:8-9
__ May 30 2 Samuel 15:23 –16:23 John 18:25–19:22 Ps. 119:113-128 Prov.16:10-11
__ May 31 2 Samuel 17:1 – 29 John 19:23 – 42 Ps. 119:129-152 Prov. 16:12-13

__ June 1 2 Samuel 18:1 – 19:10 John 20:1 – 31 Ps. 119:153-176 Prov. 16:14-15
__ June 2 2 Samuel 19:11 – 20:13 John 21:1 – 25 Ps. 120:1-7 Prov. 16:16-17
__ June 3 2 Samuel 20:14 - 22:20 Acts 1:1 – 26 Ps. 121:1-8 Prov. 16:18
__ June 4 2 Samuel 22:21 – 23:23 Acts 2:1 – 47 Ps. 122:1-9 Prov. 16:19-20
__ June 5 2 Samuel 23:24 – 24:25 Acts 3:1 – 26 Ps. 123:1-4 Prov. 16:21-23
__ June 6 1 Kings 1:1 – 53 Acts 4:1 – 37 Ps. 124:1-8 Prov. 16:24
__ June 7 1 Kings 2:1 – 3:3 Acts 5:1 – 42 Ps. 125:1-5 Prov. 16:25
__ June 8 1 Kings 3:4 – 4:34 Acts 6:1 – 15 Ps. 126:1-6 Prov. 16:26-27
__ June 9 1 Kings 5:1 – 6:38 Acts 7:1 – 29 Ps. 127:1-5 Prov. 16:28-30
__ June 10 1 Kings 7:1 – 51 Acts 7:30 – 50 Ps. 128:1-6 Prov. 16:31-33
__ June 11 1 Kings 8:1 – 66 Acts 7:51 – 8:13 Ps. 129:1-8 Prov. 17:1
__ June 12 1 Kings 9:1 – 10:29 Acts 8:14 – 40 Ps. 130:1-8 Prov. 17:2-3
__ June 13 1 Kings 11:1 – 12:19 Acts 9:1 – 25 Ps. 131:1-3 Prov. 17:4-5
__ June 14 1 Kings 12:20 – 13:34 Acts 9:26 – 43 Ps. 132:1-18 Prov. 17:6
__ June 15 1 Kings 14:1 – 15:24 Acts 10:1 – 23a Ps. 133:1-3 Prov. 17:7-8
__ June 16 1 Kings 15:25 – 17:24 Acts 10:23b – 48 Ps. 134:1-3 Prov. 17:9-11
__ June 17 1 Kings 18:1 – 46 Acts 11:1 – 30 Ps. 135:1-21 Prov. 17:12-13
__ June 18 1 Kings 19:1-21 Acts 12:1-23 Ps. 136:1-26 Prov. 17:14-15
__ June 19 1 Kings 20:1 – 21:29 Acts 12:24 – 13:15 Ps. 137:1-9 Prov. 17:16
__ June 20 1 Kings 22:1 – 53 Acts 13:16 – 41 Ps. 138:1-8 Prov. 17:17-18
__ June 21 2 Kings 1:1 – 2:25 Acts 13:42 – 14:7 Ps. 139:1-24 Prov. 17:19-21
__ June 22 2 Kings 3:1 – 4:17 Acts 14:8 – 28 Ps. 140:1-13 Prov. 17:22
__ June 23 2 Kings 4:18 – 5:27 Acts 15: 1 – 35 Ps. 141:1-10 Prov. 17:23
__ June 24 2 Kings 6:1 – 7:20 Acts 15:36 – 16:15 Ps. 142:1-7 Prov. 17:24-25
__ June 25 2 Kings 8:1 – 9:13 Acts 16:16 – 40 Ps. 143:1-12 Prov. 17:26
__ June 26 2 Kings 9:14 – 10:31 Acts 17:1 – 34 Ps. 144:1-15 Prov. 17:27-28
__ June 27 2 Kings 10:32 – 12:21 Acts 18:1-22 Ps. 145:1-21 Prov. 18:1
__ June 28 2 Kings 13:1 – 14:29 Acts 18:23 – 19:12 Ps. 146:1-10 Prov. 18:2-3
__ June 29 2 Kings 15:1 – 16:20 Acts 19:13 – 41 Ps. 147:1-20 Prov. 18:4-5
__ June 30 2 Kings 17:1 – 18:12 Acts 20:1 – 38 Ps. 148:1-14 Prov. 18:6-7

__ July 1 2 Kings 18:13 – 19:37 Acts 21:1 – 16 Ps. 149:1-9 Prov. 18:8
__ July 2 2 Kings 20:1 – 22:2 Acts 21:17 – 36 Ps. 150:1-6 Prov. 18:9-10
__ July 3 2 Kings 22:3 – 23:30 Acts 21:37 – 22:16 Ps. 1:1-6 Prov. 18:11-12
__ July 4 2 Kings 23:31 – 25:30 Acts 22:17 – 23:10 Ps. 2:1-12 Prov. 18:13
__ July 5 1 Chronicles 1:1 – 2:17 Acts 23:11 – 35 Ps. 3:1-8 Prov. 18:14-15
__ July 6 1 Chronicles 2:18 – 4:4 Acts 24:1 – 27 Ps. 4:1-8 Prov. 18:16-18
__ July 7 1 Chronicles 4:5 – 5:17 Acts 25:1 – 27 Ps. 5:1-12 Prov. 18:19
__ July 8 1 Chronicles 5:18 – 6:81 Acts 26:1 – 32 Ps. 6:1-10 Prov. 18:20-21
__ July 9 1 Chronicles 7:1 8:40 Acts 27:1 – 20 Ps. 7:1 – 17 Prov. 18:22
__ July 10 1 Chronicles 9:1 – 10:14 Acts 27:21 – 44 Ps. 8:1-9 Prov. 18:23-24
__ July 11 1 Chronicles 11:1 –12:18 Acts 28:1 – 31 Ps. 9:1-12 Prov. 19:1-3
__ July 12 1 Chronicles 12:19 –14:17 Romans 1:1 – 17 Ps. 9:13-20 Prov. 19:4-5
__ July 13 1 Chronicles 15:1 – 16:36 Romans 1:18 – 32 Ps. 10:1-15 Prov. 19:6-7
__ July 14 1 Chronicles 16:37 –18:17 Romans 2:1 – 24 Ps. 10:16-18 Prov. 19:8-9
__ July 15 1 Chronicles 19:1 – 21:30 Romans 2:25 – 3:8 Ps. 11:1-7 Prov. 19:10-12
__ July 16 1 Chronicles 22:1 –23:32 Romans 3:9 – 31 Ps. 12:1-8 Prov.19:13-14
__ July 17 1 Chronicles 24:1 – 26:11 Romans 4:1 – 12 Ps. 13:1-6 Prov. 19:15-16
__ July 18 1 Chronicles 26:12 –27:34 Romans 4:13 – 5:5 Ps. 14:1-7 Prov. 19:17
__ July 19 1 Chronicles 28:1 – 29:30 Romans 5:6 – 21 Ps. 15:1-5 Prov. 19:18-19
__ July 20 2 Chronicles 1:1 – 3:17 Romans 6:1 – 23 Ps. 16:1-11 Prov. 19:20-21
__ July 21 2 Chronicles 4:1 – 6:11 Romans 7:1 – 13 Ps. 17:1-15 Prov. 19:22-23
__ July 22 2 Chronicles 6:12 – 8:10 Romans 7:14 – 8:8 Ps. 18:1-15 Prov. 19:24-25
__ July 23 2 Chronicles 8:11 – 10:19 Romans 8:9 – 21 Ps. 18:16-36 Prov. 19:26
__ July 24 2 Chronicles 11:1 – 13:22 Romans 8:22 – 39 Ps. 18:37-50 Prov. 19:27-29
__ July 25 2 Chronicles 14:1 – 16:14 Romans 9:1 – 21 Ps. 19:1-14 Prov. 20:1
__ July 26 2 Chronicles 17:1 – 18:34 Romans 9:22 – 10:13 Ps. 20:1-9 Prov. 20:2-3
__ July 27 2 Chronicles 19:1 – 20:37 Romans 10:14 –11:12 Ps. 21:1-13 Prov. 20:4-6
__ July 28 2 Chronicles 21:1 – 23:21 Romans 11:13 – 36 Ps. 22:1-18 Prov. 20:7
__ July 29 2 Chronicles 24:1 – 25:28 Romans 12:1 – 21 Ps. 22:19-31 Prov. 20:8-10
__ July 30 2 Chronicles 26:1 – 28:27 Romans 13:1 – 14 Ps. 23:1-6 Prov. 20:11
__ July 31 2 Chronicles 29:1 – 36 Romans 14:1 – 23 Ps. 24:1-10 Prov. 20:12

__ Aug. 1 2 Chronicles 30:1 – 31:21 Romans 15:1 – 22 Ps. 25:1-15 Prov. 20:13-15
__ Aug. 2 2 Chronicles 32:1–33:13 Romans 15:23–16:7 Ps.25:16-22 Prov. 20:16-18
__ Aug. 3 2 Chronicles 33:14 –34:33 Romans 16:8 – 27 Ps. 26:1-12 Prov. 20:19
__ Aug. 4 2 Chronicles 35:1 – 36:23 1 Corinthians 1:1-17 Ps. 27:1-6 Prov. 20:20-21
__ Aug. 5 Ezra 1:1 – 2:70 1 Corinthians 1:18 -2:5 Ps. 27:7-14 Prov. 20:22-23
__ Aug. 6 Ezra 3:1 – 4:24 1 Corinthians 2:6 –3:4 Ps. 28:1-9 Prov. 20:24-25
__ Aug. 7 Ezra 5:1 – 6:22 1 Corinthians 3:5 - 23 Ps. 29:1-11 Prov. 20:26-27
__ Aug. 8 Ezra 7:1 – 8:20 1 Corinthians 4:1 – 21 Ps. 30:1-12 Prov. 20:28-30
__ Aug. 9 Ezra 8:21 – 9:15 1 Corinthians 5:1 – 13 Ps. 31:1-8 Prov. 21:1-2

__ Aug. 10 Ezra 10:1 – 44 1 Corinthians 6:1 - 20 Ps. 31:9-18 Prov. 21:3

__ Aug. 11 Nehemiah 1:1 – 3:14 1Corinthians 7:1 – 24 Ps. 31:19-24 Prov. 21:4

__ Aug. 12 Nehemiah 3:15 – 5:13 1Corinthians 7:25 – 40 Ps. 32:1-11 Prov. 21:5-7

__ Aug. 13 Nehemiah 5:14 – 7:60 1Corinthians 8:1 – 13 Ps. 33:1-11 Prov. 21:8-10

__ Aug. 14 Nehemiah 7:61–9:21 1Corinthians 9:1–18 Ps. 33:12-22 Prov. 21:11-12

__ Aug. 15 Nehemiah 9:22–10:39 1Corinthians 9:19–10:13 Ps.34:1-10 Prov. 21:13

__ Aug. 16 Nehemiah 11:1–12:26 1Corinthians 10:14-11:2 Ps.34:11-22 Prov.21:14-16

__ Aug. 17 Nehemiah 12:27 – 13:31 1 Corinthians 11:3 – 16 Ps. 35:1-16 Prov. 21:17-18

__ Aug. 18 Esther 1:1 – 3:15 1 Corinthians 11:7 – 34 Ps. 35:17-28 Prov. 21:19-20

__ Aug. 19 Esther 4:1 – 7:10 1 Corinthians 12:1 – 26 Ps. 36:1-12 Prov. 21:21-22

__ Aug. 20 Esther 8:1 – 10:3 1 Corinthians12:27 –13:13 Ps. 37:1-11 Prov. 21:23-24

__ Aug. 21 Job 1:1 – 3:26 1 Corinthians 14:1 – 17 Ps. 37:12-29 Prov. 21:25-26

__ Aug. 22 Job 4:1 – 7:21 1 Corinthians 14:18 –40 Ps. 37:30-40 Prov. 21:27

__ Aug. 23 Job 8:1 – 11:20 1 Corinthians 15:1 – 28 Ps. 38:1-22 Prov. 21:28-29

__ Aug. 24 Job 12:1 – 15:35 1 Corinthians 15:29 – 58 Ps. 39:1-13 Prov. 21:30-31

__ Aug. 25 Job 16:1 – 19:29 1 Corinthians 16:1 – 24 Ps. 40:1-10 Prov. 22:1

__ Aug. 26 Job 20:1 – 22:30 2 Corinthians 1:1 – 11 Ps. 40:11-17 Prov. 22:2-4

__ Aug. 27 Job 23:1 – 27:23 2 Corinthians 1:12 – 2:11 Ps. 41:1–13 Prov. 22:5-6

__ Aug. 28 Job 28:1 – 30:31 2 Corinthians 2:12 – 17 Ps. 42:1–11 Prov. 22:7

__ Aug. 29 Job 31:1 – 33:33 2 Corinthians 3:1 – 18 Ps. 43:1–5 Prov. 22:8-9

__ Aug. 30 Job 34:1 – 36:33 2 Corinthians 4:1 – 12 Ps. 44:1-8 Prov. 22:10-12

__ Aug. 31 Job 37:1 – 39:30 2 Corinthians 4:13 –5:10 Ps. 44:9-26 Prov. 22:13

__ Sept. 1 Job 40:1 – 42:17 2 Corinthians 5:11 –21 Ps. 45:1-17 Prov. 22:14

__ Sept. 2 Ecclesiastes 1:1 – 3:22 2 Corinthians 6:1-13 Ps. 46:1-11 Prov. 22:15

__ Sept. 3 Ecclesiastes 4:1 – 6:12 2 Corinthians 6:14 – 7:7 Ps. 47:1-9 Prov. 22:16

__ Sept. 4 Ecclesiastes 7:1 - 9:18 2 Corinthians 7:8 – 16 Ps. 48:1-14 Prov. 22:17-19

__ Sept. 5 Ecclesiastes 10:1 –12:14 2 Corinthians 8:1–15 Ps. 49:1 –20 Prov.22:20-21

__ Sept. 6 Song of Songs 1:1 – 4:16 2 Corinthians 8:16 – 24 Ps. 50:1-23 Prov. 22:22-23

__ Sept. 7 Song of Songs 5:1 – 8:14 2 Corinthians 9:1 – 15 Ps. 51:1-19 Prov. 22:24-25

__ Sept. 8 Isaiah 1:1 – 2:22 2 Corinthians 10:1 – 18 Ps. 52:1-9 Prov. 22:26-27

__ Sept. 9 Isaiah 3:1 – 5:30 2 Corinthians 11:1 – 15 Ps. 53:1-6 Prov. 22:28-29

__ Sept. 10 Isaiah 6:1 – 7:25 2 Corinthians 11:16 – 33 Ps. 54:1-7 Prov. 23:1-3

__ Sept. 11 Isaiah 8:1 – 9:21 2 Corinthians 12:1 – 10 Ps. 55:1-23 Prov. 23:4-5

__ Sept. 12 Isaiah 10:1 – 11:16 2 Corinthians 12:11 – 21 Ps. 56:1-13 Prov. 23:6-8

__ Sept. 13 Isaiah 12:1 – 14:32 2 Corinthians 13:1 – 14 Ps. 57:1-11 Prov. 23:9-11

__ Sept. 14 Isaiah 15:1 – 18:7 Galatians 1:1 – 24 Ps. 58:1-11 Prov. 23:12

__ Sept. 15 Isaiah 19:1 – 21:17 Galatians 2:1 – 16 Ps. 59:1-17 Prov. 23:13-14

__ Sept. 16 Isaiah 22:1 – 24:23 Galatians 2:17 – 3:9 Ps. 60:1-12 Prov. 23:15-16

__ Sept. 17 Isaiah 25:1 – 28:13 Galatians 3:10 – 22 Ps. 61:1-8 Prov. 23:17-18

__ Sept. 18 Isaiah 28:14 – 30:11 Galatians 3:23 – 4:31 Ps. 62:1-12 Prov. 23:19-21

__ Sept. 19 Isaiah 30:12 – 33:12 Galatians 5:1 – 12 Ps. 63:1-11 Prov. 23:22
__ Sept. 20 Isaiah 33:13 – 36:22 Galatians 5:13 – 26 Ps. 64:1-10 Prov. 23:23
__ Sept. 21 Isaiah 37:1 – 38:22 Galatians 6:1 – 18 Ps. 65:1-13 Prov. 23:24-25
__ Sept. 22 Isaiah 39:1 – 41:16 Ephesians 1:1 – 23 Ps. 66:1-20 Prov. 23:26-28
__ Sept. 23 Isaiah 41:17 – 43:13 Ephesians 2:1 – 22 Ps. 67:1-7 Prov. 23:29-35
__ Sept. 24 Isaiah 43:14 – 45:10 Ephesians 3:1 – 21 Ps. 68:1-18 Prov. 24:1-2
__ Sept. 25 Isaiah 45:11 – 48:11 Ephesians 4:1 – 16 Ps. 68:19-35 Prov. 24:3-4
__ Sept. 26 Isaiah 48:12 – 50:11 Ephesians 4:17 – 32 Ps. 69:1-18 Prov. 24:5-6
__ Sept. 27 Isaiah 51:1 – 53:12 Ephesians 5:1 – 33 Ps. 69:19-36 Prov. 24:7
__ Sept. 28 Isaiah 54:1 – 57:13 Ephesians 6:1 – 24 Ps. 70:1-5 Prov. 24:8
__ Sept. 29 Isaiah 57:14 – 59:21 Philippians 1:1 –26 Ps. 71:1-24 Prov. 24:9-10
__ Sept. 30 Isaiah 60:1 – 62:5 Philippians 1:27 – 2:18 Ps. 72:1-20 Prov. 24:11-12

__ Oct. 1 Isaiah 62:6 – 65:25 Philippians 2:19 – 3:4a Ps. 73:1-28 Prov. 24:13-14
__ Oct. 2 Isaiah 66:1 – 24 Philippians 3:4b – 21 Ps. 74:1-23 Prov. 24:15-16
__ Oct. 3 Jeremiah 1:1 – 2:30 Philippians 4:1 – 23 Ps. 75:1-10 Prov. 24:17-20
__ Oct. 4 Jeremiah 2:31 – 4:18 Colossians 1:1 – 20 Ps. 76:1-12 Prov. 24:21-22
__ Oct. 5 Jeremiah 4:19 – 6:14 Colossians 1:21 – 2:7 Ps. 77:1-20 Prov. 24:23-25
__ Oct. 6 Jeremiah 6:15 – 8:7 Colossians 2:8 – 23 Ps. 78:1-31 Prov. 24:26
__ Oct. 7 Jeremiah 8:8 – 9:26 Colossians 3:1 – 17 Ps. 78:32-55 Prov. 24:27
__ Oct. 8 Jeremiah 10:1 – 11:23 Colossians 3:18 – 4:18 Ps. 78:56-72 Prov. 24:28-29
__ Oct. 9 Jeremiah 12:1 – 14:10 1 Thess. 1:1 – 2:9 Ps. 79:1-13 Prov. 24:30-34
__ Oct. 10 Jeremiah 14:11 – 16:15 1 Thess. 2:10 – 3:13 Ps. 80:1-19 Prov. 25:1-5
__ Oct. 11 Jeremiah 16:16 – 18:23 1 Thess. 4:1 – 5:3 Ps. 81:1-16 Prov. 25:6-7
__ Oct. 12 Jeremiah 19:1 – 21:14 1 Thess. 5:4 – 28 Ps. 82:1-8 Prov. 25:8-10
__ Oct. 13 Jeremiah 22:1 – 23:20 2 Thess. 1:1 – 12 Ps. 83:1 – 18 Prov. 25:11-14
__ Oct. 14 Jeremiah 23:21 – 25:38 2 Thess. 2:1 – 17 Ps. 84:1-12 Prov. 25:15
__ Oct. 15 Jeremiah 26:1 – 27:22 2 Thess. 3:1 – 18 Ps. 85:1-13 Prov. 25:16
__ Oct. 16 Jeremiah 28:1 – 29:32 1 Timothy 1:1 – 20 Ps. 86:1-17 Prov. 25:17
__ Oct. 17 Jeremiah 30:1 – 31:26 1 Timothy 2:1 – 15 Ps. 87:1-7 Prov. 25:18-19
__ Oct. 18 Jeremiah 31:27 – 32:44 1 Timothy 3:1 – 16 Ps. 88:1-18 Prov. 25:20-22
__ Oct. 19 Jeremiah 33:1 – 34:22 1 Timothy 4:1 – 16 Ps. 89:1-13 Prov. 25:23-24
__ Oct. 20 Jeremiah 35:1 – 36:32 1 Timothy 5:1 – 25 Ps. 89:14-37 Prov. 25:25-27
__ Oct. 21 Jeremiah 37:1 – 38:28 1 Timothy 6:1 – 21 Ps. 89:38-52 Prov. 25:28
__ Oct. 22 Jeremiah 39:1 – 41:18 2 Timothy 1:1 – 18 Ps. 90:1 – 91:16 Prov. 26:1-2
__ Oct. 23 Jeremiah 42:1 – 44:23 2 Timothy 2:1 – 21 Ps. 92:1–93:5 Prov. 26:3-5
__ Oct. 24 Jeremiah 44:24 – 47:7 2 Timothy 2:22 – 3:17 Ps. 94:1-23 Prov. 26:6-8
__ Oct. 25 Jeremiah 48:1 – 49:22 2 Timothy 4:1 –22 Ps. 95:1 – 96:13 Prov. 26:9-12
__ Oct. 26 Jeremiah 49:23 – 50:46 Titus 1:1 – 16 Ps. 97:1 – 98:9 Prov. 26:13-16
__ Oct. 27 Jeremiah 51:1 – 53 Titus 2:1 – 15 Ps. 99:1-9 Prov. 26:17
__ Oct. 28 Jeremiah 51:54 – 52:34 Titus 3:1 – 15 Ps. 100:1-5 Prov. 26:18-19

__ Oct. 29 Lamentations 1:1 – 2:19 Philemon 1:1 – 25 Ps. 101:1-8 Prov. 26:20
__ Oct. 30 Lamentations 2:20 –3:66 Hebrews 1:1 – 14 Ps. 102:1-28 Prov. 26:21-22
__ Oct. 31 Lamentations 4:1 – 5:22 Hebrews 2:1 – 18 Ps. 103:1-22 Prov. 26:23

__ Nov. 1 Ezekiel 1:1 – 3:15 Hebrews 3:1 – 19 Ps. 104:1 -23 Prov. 26:24-26
__ Nov. 2 Ezekiel 3:16 – 6:14 Hebrews 4:1 – 16 Ps. 104:24 -25 Prov. 26:27
__ Nov. 3 Ezekiel 7:1 – 9:11 Hebrews 5:1 – 14 Ps. 105:1 – 15 Prov. 26:28
__ Nov. 4 Ezekiel 10:1 – 11:25 Hebrews 6:1 – 20 Ps. 105:16 -36 Prov. 27:1-2
__ Nov. 5 Ezekiel 12:1 – 14:11 Hebrews 7:1 – 17 Ps. 105:37 -45 Prov. 27:3
__ Nov. 6 Ezekiel 14:12 – 16:42 Hebrews 7:18 – 28 Ps. 106:1 – 12 Prov. 27:4-6
__ Nov. 7 Ezekiel 16:43 – 17:24 Hebrews 8:1 – 13 Ps. 106:13 –31 Prov. 27:7-9
__ Nov. 8 Ezekiel 18:1 – 19:14 Hebrews 9:1 – 10 Ps. 106:32 – 48 Prov. 27:10
__ Nov. 9 Ezekiel 20:1 – 49 Hebrews 9:11 – 28 Ps. 107:1 – 43 Prov. 27:11
__ Nov. 10 Ezekiel 21:1 – 22:31 Hebrews 10:1 – 17 Ps. 108:1 – 13 Prov. 27:12
__ Nov. 11 Ezekiel 23:1 – 49 Hebrews 10:18 – 39 Ps. 109:1 – 31 Prov. 27:13
__ Nov. 12 Ezekiel 24:1 – 26:21 Hebrews 11:1 – 16 Ps. 110:1 - 7 Prov. 27:14
__ Nov. 13 Ezekiel 27:1 – 28:26 Hebrews 11:17 – 31 Ps. 111:1 – 10 Prov. 27:15-16
__ Nov. 14 Ezekiel 29:1 – 30:26 Hebrews 11:32 –12:13 Ps. 112:1- 10 Prov. 27:17
__ Nov. 15 Ezekiel 31:1 – 32:32 Hebrews 12:14–29 Ps. 113:1–114:8 Prov.27:18-20
__ Nov. 16 Ezekiel 33:1 – 34:31 Hebrews 13:1 – 25 Ps. 115:1-18 Prov. 27:21-22
__ Nov. 17 Ezekiel 35:1 – 36:38 James 1:1-18 Ps. 116:1-19 Prov. 27:23-27
__ Nov. 18 Ezekiel 37:1 – 38:23 James 1:19 – 2:17 Ps. 117:1-2 Prov. 28:1
__ Nov. 19 Ezekiel 39:1 – 40:27 James 2:18 – 3:18 Ps. 118:1-18 Prov. 28:2
__ Nov. 20 Ezekiel 40:28 – 41:26 James 4:1 –17 Ps. 118:19-29 Prov. 28:3-5
__ Nov. 21 Ezekiel 42:1 – 43:27 James 5:1 – 20 Ps. 119:1 – 16 Prov. 28:6-7
__ Nov. 22 Ezekiel 44:1 – 45:12 1 Peter 1:1 – 12 Ps. 119:17-32 Prov. 28:8-10
__ Nov. 23 Ezekiel 45:13 – 46:24 1 Peter 1:13 – 2:10 Ps. 119:33-48 Prov. 28:11
__ Nov. 24 Ezekiel 47:1 – 48:35 1 Peter 2:11 – 3:7 Ps. 119:49-64 Prov. 28:12-13
__ Nov. 25 Daniel 1:1 – 2:23 1 Peter 3:8 – 4:6 Ps. 119:65-80 Prov. 28:14
__ Nov. 26 Daniel 2:24 – 3:30 1 Peter 4:7 – 5:14 Ps. 119:81-96 Prov. 28:15-16
__ Nov. 27 Daniel 4:1 – 37 2 Peter 1:1 – 21 Ps. 119:97-112 Prov. 28:17-18
__ Nov. 28 Daniel 5:1 – 31 2 Peter 2:1 – 22 Ps. 119:113-128 Prov. 28:19-20
__ Nov. 29 Daniel 6:1 – 28 2 Peter 3:1 – 18 Ps. 119:129-152 Prov. 28:21-22
__ Nov. 30 Daniel 7:1 – 28 1 John 1:1 – 10 Ps. 119:153-176 Prov. 28:23-24

__ Dec. 1 Daniel 8:1 – 27 1 John 2:1 – 17 Ps. 120:1-7 Prov. 28:25-26
__ Dec. 2 Daniel 9:1 – 11:1 1 John 2:18 – 3:6 Ps. 121:1-8 Prov. 28:27-28
__ Dec. 3 Daniel 11:2 – 35 1 John 3:7 – 24 Ps. 122:1-9 Prov. 29:1
__ Dec. 4 Daniel 11:36 – 12:13 1 John 4:1 – 21 Ps. 123:1-4 Prov. 29:2-4
__ Dec. 5 Hosea 1:1 – 3:5 1 John 5:1 – 21 Ps. 124:1-8 Prov. 29:5-8

___ Dec. 6 Hosea 4:1 – 5:15 2 John 1:1 – 13 Ps. 125:1-5 Prov. 29:9-11
___ Dec. 7 Hosea 6:1 – 9:17 3 John 1:1 – 14 Ps. 126:1-6 Prov. 29:12-14
___ Dec. 8 Hosea 10:1 –14:9 Jude 1:1-25 Ps. 127:1-5 Prov. 29:15-17
___ Dec. 9 Joel 1:1 – 3:21 Revelation 1:1 - 20 Ps. 128:1-6 Prov. 29:18
___ Dec. 10 Amos 1:1 – 3:15 Revelation 2:1 –17 Ps. 129:1-8 Prov. 29:19-20
___ Dec. 11 Amos 4:1 – 6:14 Revelation 2:18 – 3:6 Ps.130:1-8 Prov. 29:21-22
___ Dec. 12 Amos 7:1 – 9:15 Revelation 3:7 – 22 Ps.131:1-3 Prov. 29:23
___ Dec. 13 Obadiah 1:1 – 21 Revelation 4:1 – 11 Ps.132 1-18 Prov. 29:24-25
___ Dec. 14 Jonah 1:1 – 4:11 Revelation 5:1 – 14 Ps.133:1-3 Prov. 29:26-27
___ Dec. 15 Micah 1:1 – 4:13 Revelation 6:1 – 17 Ps.134:1-3 Prov. 30:1-4
___ Dec. 16 Micah 5:1 – 7:20 Revelation 7:1 – 17 Ps.135:1-21 Prov. 30:5-6
___ Dec. 17 Nahum 1:1 3:19 Revelation 8:1 – 13 Ps.136:1-26 Prov. 30:7-9
___ Dec. 18 Habakkuk 1:1 – 3:19 Revelation 9:1 – 21 Ps.137:1-9 Prov. 30:10
___ Dec. 19 Zephaniah 1:1 – 3:20 Revelation 10:1 – 11 Ps.138:1-8 Prov. 30:11-14
___ Dec. 20 Haggai 1:1 – 2:23 Revelation 11:1 – 19 Ps.139:1-24 Prov. 30:15-16
___ Dec. 21 Zechariah 1:1 – 21 Revelation 12:1 – 13:1a Ps.140:1-13 Prov. 30:17
___ Dec. 22 Zechariah 2:1 – 3:10 Revelation 13:1b – 18 Ps.141:1-10 Prov. 30:18-20
___ Dec. 23 Zechariah 4:1 – 5:11 Revelation 14:1 – 20 Ps.142:1-7 Prov. 30:21-23
___ Dec. 24 Zechariah 6:1 – 7:14 Revelation 15:1 - 8 Ps.143:1-12 Prov. 30:24-28
___ Dec. 25 Zechariah 8:1 – 23 Revelation 16:1 – 21 Ps.144:1-15 Prov. 30:29-31
___ Dec. 26 Zechariah 9:1 – 17 Revelation 17:1 – 18 Ps.145:1-21 Prov. 30:32
___ Dec. 27 Zechariah 10:1 – 11:17 Revelation 18:1 – 24 Ps.146:1-10 Prov. 30:33
___ Dec. 28 Zechariah 12:1 – 13:9 Revelation 19:1 – 21 Ps.147:1-20 Prov. 31:1-7
___ Dec. 29 Zechariah 14:1 – 21 Revelation 20:1 – 15 Ps.148:1-14 Prov. 31:8-9
___ Dec. 30 Malachi 1:1 – 2:17 Revelation 21:1 – 27 Ps.149:1-9 Prov. 31:10-24
___ Dec. 31 Malachi 3:1 – 4:6 Revelation 22:1 – 21 Ps.150:1-6 Prov. 31:25-31